This journal belongs to:

....

If found, please contact:

....

BuzzFeed

GUIDED TRAVEL JOURNAL

A Place to Record Your Experiences,
Adventures, and Inspirations

PHILADELPHIA

The findings, views, and recommendations expressed herein are not the responsibility of and do not necessarily reflect the view of BuzzFeed, Inc.

Copyright © 2022 by BuzzFeed, Inc. All rights reserved.

Hachette Book Group supports the right to free expression and the value of copyright. The purpose of copyright is to encourage writers and artists to produce the creative works that enrich our culture.

The scanning, uploading, and distribution of this book without permission is a theft of the author's intellectual property. If you would like permission to use material from the book (other than for review purposes), please contact permissions@hbgusa.com. Thank you for your support of the author's rights.

RP Studio™
Hachette Book Group
1290 Avenue of the Americas, New York, NY 10104
www.runningpress.com
@Running_Press

Printed in Singapore

First Edition: June 2022

Published by RP Studio, an imprint of Perseus Books, LLC,
a subsidiary of Hachette Book Group, Inc.
The RP Studio name and logo is a trademark of the Hachette Book Group.

The publisher is not responsible for websites (or their content) that are not owned by the publisher.

Design by Joshua McDonnell
Illustrations by Jay Fleckenstein, Michael Kilian, and Ivy Tai

ISBN: 978-0-7624-7496-7

COS

10 9 8 7 6 5 4 3 2 1

CONTENTS

INTRODUCTION	7
BRING ME! TRAVEL COMMANDMENTS	9
TRAVEL TIPS AND HACKS	14
Packing	15
Lodging	16
Transportation	17
Safety	18
Budgeting	20
Eco-Conscious Travel	22
MY ULTIMATE BUCKET LIST	27
THE PLACES I'VE VISITED	38
EAT	40
SEE	60
DO	83
MEET	103
TRIP PLANNING AND REFLECTIONS	119
ADJECTIVE WHEELS	168

INTRODUCTION

There's something special about putting pen to paper and writing about where you went, what you did, what you ate, what you saw, and how you felt. Sure, you can take a million photos to document your travels, too, but journaling helps you dig a little deeper and remember all those big and small feelings about moments and memories in time, something a photo can't always quite capture. It's also something to refer to the next time you plan a trip and it's a way to revisit your amazing adventures when you're back home and feeling all wanderlusty. And, if you're lucky enough to have a journey filled with once-in-a-lifetime experiences, you're going to want to make sure you can remember everything about that trip forever.

BuzzFeed launched *Bring Me!* in 2017 (aka the *Before Times*) as a way for people to discover unique things to do, places to eat, and sights to see around the world. And despite all the unexpected changes in the last couple of years, this mission still rings true. Now that we're finding it safer to travel again, we're all itching to get up and go! After all, whether you're venturing near or far, across the ocean or only a few hours away, traveling is therapeutic and extraordinary.

Thank you for choosing this guided journal as a companion for your trips. We hope it helps you plan your adventures, see your travels in a different way, or discover something new about yourself or the world around you. We also encourage you to use the pocket in the back of this journal for saving mementos, receipts, tickets, and more. This journal is a companion to *BuzzFeed Bring Me!: A Travel-Lover's Guide to the World's Most Unlikely Destinations, Remarkable Experiences, and Spectacular Sights*, which we encourage you to read if you're looking for some exciting ideas for things to see and experience around the globe.

Happy traveling!

HOW TO USE THIS JOURNAL

These pages are a container for your travel dreams, observations, and memories. Plot your ultimate travel bucket lists and jot down all the best things you eat, see, and do on your adventures in a way that's easy to refer back to when your friends ask you to share your travel tips. Then, in the planning section, you'll find space to document each trip and pages with writing prompts to help you reflect and record all aspects of your journey. If you're feeling stuck for words, check out the adjective wheels on p. 168 for writing inspiration.

BRING ME! TRAVEL COMMANDMENTS

Just as there's no one right way to plan a trip, there's also no one right way to take one. But whether we're staying local or flying to the other side of the globe, these are the ten principles we always try to follow when we travel. You can follow them, too, or you can choose to ignore them, but, either way, we hope they'll inspire you to think of your own personal travel commandments.

1. **Be Kind to the Environment**

    It might sound obvious, but travel can have a devastating impact on the planet. So the more you can do to minimize your environmental impact while traveling, the better. Consider following the principles of Leave No Trace (find them at www.lnt.org) when you're visiting the great outdoors. Bring your own reusable water bottle to refill on your travels and don't leave the lights on in your hotel room when you're not there (just 'cause you're not paying the electricity bill doesn't mean it "doesn't count"). There are countless ways to make small, conscious choices to decrease your carbon footprint while you're exploring this beautiful Earth we all call home.

2. **Be Curious**

    You can spend months (years!) reading, watching, and absorbing information about a destination, but nothing compares to what you'll learn once you're actually there. Strike up a conversation with your taxi driver, speak to locals about their favorite spots, and ask your fellow travelers for their tips. Follow your curiosity—you never know where it might lead you.

3. Don't Be a Hater

We get it: Travel can be stressful and it doesn't always bring out the best in us. But even in the most unfortunate situations, focusing on the good instead of the bad can go a long way. Negative energy radiates and won't just affect your trip—it'll also drag down the experience of people around you. It's totally fine to be annoyed every now and again, but have a quick vent, take a few deep breaths, and let it go. No one wants to travel with a hater.

4. Support Local Businesses

One of the best things you can do to support the economy and people of a place you visit is to shop locally. So take that extra step to research and see if the store, restaurant, or other place of business you're patronizing is actually owned by locals. Even better, try to support small businesses that are owned by traditionally marginalized groups in the community.

5. Get Comfortable with Being Uncomfortable

And we don't just mean on a long-haul flight. Visiting new places, meeting new people, and trying new things can feel strange and scary at times, but stepping out of your comfort zone and engaging with different people, places, and things is how you grow. Traveling and learning about other cultures through firsthand experiences is a huge privilege, so be thankful and make the most of it. If you wanted to be comfortable, you'd have stayed on the couch.

6. Be Empathetic

One of the best parts of traveling is the people you meet. Wherever you go in the world, you're probably going to interact with people from varied cultures, whose life experiences are vastly different from yours. Leave your judgment at home with that fifth pair of shoes you *definitely* won't need and embrace the opportunity to better understand the experience of others.

7. **Embrace the Unexpected**

    You can plan your entire trip to a tee, but some of the best moments you have traveling are going to be completely unplanned and spontaneous. So don't be afraid to diverge from your itinerary every once in a while and say yes to something different if the opportunity presents itself, because these are usually the experiences that end up as the most memorable parts of your trip.

8. **Health above All Else**

    If there's one thing you *should* definitely plan ahead for, it's your health. Make sure you're prepared for any personal or public health emergency. Travel insurance that covers you in case you get sick while traveling is usually a good idea, as is researching the local health hazards and medical care options at any place you're visiting. Learn how to ask for help in the local language and take note of the emergency phone numbers in each country you visit; remember, only a fraction of the world uses 911.

9. **Remember, It's Not All about You**

    Sometimes it's easy to forget that nearly every place you visit—no matter how much it seems to cater to tourists—is also somebody else's home. When traveling, always remember that not everyone is here to make sure you have an enjoyable trip and not everyone speaks the same language you do. And that's okay. Always be respectful of other people's spaces and communities.

10. **Do It for the Memories**

    Don't get us wrong, we're all for snapping pics and documenting travels, but it can be easy to get so caught up trying to take the perfect shot that you forget to really take in the experience. You didn't travel all that way to look at the world through *another* screen, so remember to put your camera down every now and then and enjoy the moment.

MY TRAVEL COMMANDMENTS

Okay, now it's your turn! Think about your beliefs, values, and what's important to you while traveling, then write a few of your own intentions for your trip.

"Nothing lasts forever, except the day before you start your vacation."

—Unknown

TRAVEL TIPS AND HACKS

If you ask us, planning a trip is half the fun—the anticipation of all the new places you're going to visit and all the cool things you're going to see can be incredibly exciting. But it's also time-consuming, and along with the buildup comes pressure to make everything *perfect* and get the most out of your hard-earned cash. Where to go? Where to stay? What to pack? So many decisions!

The reality is, no trip is ever going to be perfect—travel is inherently messy and unpredictable—and that's what makes it so interesting. That said, there are still plenty of ways you can be a savvy traveler whether you're embarking on your first trip or your fiftieth.

PACKING

You either love it or hate it. While it definitely helps to be prepared, these days you can pick up most essentials in any country you visit (so don't panic if you forget your toothbrush!). Clothes will probably take up the most space in your luggage, so the biggest factor to consider is the weather. Check your destination's monthly average temperature and rainfall so you can prepare accordingly. For packing lists, flip to the "Trip Planning and Reflections" section on page 119.

In the meantime, here are a few handy packing tips:
- Instead of folding your clothes, roll them to save space in your bag. This also makes it easier to see your items so you can just grab what you need without pulling *everything* out. Pack shirts with shirts, pants with pants, underwear and socks together, etc.
- To avoid overpacking, bring some laundry detergent and a mini elastic clothesline so you can do some washing on the road.
- Opt for light layers that you can easily take off or put on, rather than big, bulky items of clothing, especially if you're packing for multiple seasons or climates.
- Invest in some reusable, leak-proof, travel-size bottles, and fill them up with your favorite bath products. It's cheaper in the long run and better for the environment. For more eco-travel tips, flip to page 22.
- Airline rules for carry-on bag sizes and liquid restrictions may vary, so be sure to check and adhere to local regulations whether you're flying domestically or internationally.

LODGING

Accommodations are so much more than just a place to rest your head at night: They can take your trip from good to great. And great doesn't always have to mean a swanky, five-star resort—it really depends on what kind of trip you're planning. Fancy hotels might be the way to go if you're plotting a romantic vacation with your SO. But if you're headed on a solo adventure, you might have more fun staying at a budget hostel where you can meet other travelers, and—who knows?—you might make a new friend or find a temporary travel companion. Or if you're cruising with the whole crew, you might want to opt for a rental with more space so you can all bunk together.

Here are a few things to keep in mind when you're planning your accommodations:

- Go beyond the city center. Staying in fringe neighborhoods (where locals actually live) can help give you a more authentic feel for the place you're visiting.
- Read the reviews! Learning about the experience of past guests is the best way to get an idea of what the property is really like.
- Nightly rates change often, so always compare prices on different booking websites before locking in your stay. Booking directly with the property can sometimes be cheaper than going through a third party.

TRANSPORTATION

You might think of transportation as a means to an end when you're traveling, but it can be just as memorable an experience as anything else on your trip. If you plan it right, this is when you get to quietly pause, sit back, and reflect on your travels (not to mention enjoy the views outside). Sure, getting around can often be the most stressful aspect of any trip, but the more time and effort you put toward researching this part in advance, the less hassle you'll have to deal with when it comes to traveling from A to B safely and smoothly.

Check out these helpful tips for getting around:
- If you're taking a taxi without a working meter, negotiate the agreed-upon price with the driver up front, and even write it down on a piece of paper that you both acknowledge as the price you'll pay for the ride.
- Always travel with licensed taxis or transport services. At airports and stations, it's best to wait for vehicles at the official taxi stands. Watch out for unmarked cars with no meters and/or no visible driver's license inside.
- If it's available, use a taxi app or rideshare service for additional peace of mind. You'll have a record of your trip and you can follow along on a map to make sure the driver is taking the most efficient route.
- If you plan to get around using a bus or subway, research the local public transportation system before you travel. Sometimes you can save money by purchasing a day tripper pass online in advance.
- Download offline maps to your phone. If you're a paper map or guidebook kind of traveler, consider hiding your map inside another book so you look less like a tourist.

SAFETY

As exciting as travel can be, it can also be daunting and sometimes even dangerous. The world is full of unknowns and no activity is 100 percent safe—but that shouldn't stop you from getting out there and exploring. We're all for stepping out of our comfort zones when we travel and we hope you are, too.

Here are some practical tips to help you have a safe and stress-free adventure:

- Do your own in-depth research about every destination and experience on your itinerary. Consult the US State Department website for travel advisories, read reviews on trusted booking sites and travel forums, and keep checking local tourism or government sites for any warnings or updates during your trip.
- Scan your passport, driver's license, any visas, etc. and send them to your email (or upload them to the cloud or put them on a flash drive) and print out a copy that you can carry with you, just in case.

- Share your travel plans with a friend or family member back home. That way someone always knows roughly where you are or where you're meant to be, in case of emergency.
- Bring a backup credit or debit card and store it in a separate bag or pocket from the rest of your money.
- Keeping a bit of cash on you can get you out of a sticky situation; for example, if the only ATM at the airport doesn't accept foreign bank cards.
- Go to the doctor's for a checkup before you travel, research potential health risks at your destinations, and get any recommended vaccinations. Oh, and don't forget your hand sanitizer.
- Figure out what level of risk you're comfortable with. Everyone has a different level of risk tolerance, so what's right for someone else might not be right for you. Be true to yourself and don't feel pressured to do anything you don't want to do.
- Consider travel insurance. No matter how well you plan, things can still go awry. If you think you'd benefit from a little peace of mind when faced with the unexpected, it might be worth taking out an insurance policy (just be sure to read the fine print carefully so you know what is and isn't covered).
- If you're traveling internationally, familiarize yourself with the country's emergency numbers and save them in your phone.
- Trust your gut. Always. You're more intuitive than you may realize.

BUDGETING

There's no denying that traveling can be expensive. From airfares to taxis to rental cars to filling your tank with gas, just the act of getting to your destination can be costly—and that's only the beginning. But while all travel costs money, there are some smart ways you can help cut down on your spending.

Here are some tips to help stretch your money further:
- Okay, this one's obvious, but it has to be said: Make a budget for your trip. It's impossible to stick to a budget if you don't even know how much money you have to spend to begin with. We know it's not fun to think about this sort of stuff on vacation, so don't worry about making it perfect. A good place to start is to work out the overall maximum cost for your trip and divide it by the number of days you're traveling to figure out an average daily spending limit.
- If you're flexible with your destination or feel like being spontaneous, plan your trip around where you can get cheap flights. Sign up for flight alerts and airline sales so you never miss a good deal.

- When you have a long distance between destinations, investigate whether there are options to travel at night. Sleeping on an overnight flight, train, or bus = saving money on a night of accommodation. (Of course, traveling after dark can be more dangerous, so you should always consider your specific situation when deciding if it's safe to do so and take extra precautions.)
- Opt for a home rental or a hostel with a kitchen so you don't have to eat out for every meal.
- Take advantage of free city walking tours. Usually run by locals, these can provide a great overview of a city and help you get your bearings when you first arrive. Just remember to tip your guide!
- Travel during the shoulder months (non-peak seasons). You might be able to score cheaper deals on flights and hotels *and* you won't have to deal with peak-season crowds. It's a total win-win.
- Get yourself a travel-specific debit or credit card. Look for cards that offer competitive exchange rates and don't charge international transaction fees.
- Many museums and galleries offer free or discounted admission days, so it's always worth researching before you go (just be aware these are often the busiest days, too). And if you're a student, make sure you pack your ID card and ask about student discounts.

ECO-CONSCIOUS TRAVEL

It's no secret that travel and tourism can have terrible consequences for the environment and local communities. Enter *ecotourism*, which is defined as "responsible travel to natural areas that conserves the environment, sustains the well-being of the local people, and involves interpretation and education." Along with prioritizing ecotourism on your trip, there are ways you can practice more eco-friendly travel every step of the way, from the moment you start planning your trip, to when you're packing your bags, to when you land at your destination. For more about ecotourism, visit www.ecotourism.org. You can also pledge to travel better at www.sustainabletravel.org.

Here are some ideas to help you be a more eco-conscious traveler:

- Look for places to stay that are committed to a low environmental and social footprint, whether that means using green energy sources or sustainable building materials. Also, try to find accommodations, tours, and other experiences that are owned and managed by—or working in partnership with—indigenous or local communities.

- Unplug big appliances before you leave home, especially older ones, which can still drain energy even when they're turned off.
- Opt for digital tickets instead of paper ones.
- If you're staying at a hotel, ask if you can opt out of daily linen and towel services. Using fresh sheets and towels every day comes at a massive environmental cost.
- When you're traveling in nature, follow the principles of Leave No Trace (find them at www.lnt.org). Don't litter, and leave things as you found them.
- If you see litter—a hair tie, a plastic straw, or anything that doesn't belong—on the beach or anywhere else in nature, pick it up! You'll make the place more beautiful and can feel good knowing that you might have saved an animal from an uncomfortable or life-threatening situation.
- Heading to the beach? Pack an ocean-friendly sunscreen, because regular sunscreen can cause coral bleaching and other damage to marine life.
- Bring your own meal kit to avoid single-use plastics when you're eating out. You can pack your own spork and a cloth napkin and even a collapsible food container to take those leftovers back to the hotel. Don't forget to bring a reusable water bottle, too!
- Buy a set of refillable containers for your toiletries (or reuse small jars and tins you already have!). Also, just say no to the mini travel-sized toiletries at hotels. We know they're cute, but all that single-use plastic packaging can really hurt the environment.
- Stash a reusable tote bag in your suitcase. It's one less plastic bag you'll need to ask for when you're souvenir shopping.

Your turn! Use this space to write down your own travel commandments, tips and hacks, or ideas for traveling more responsibly.

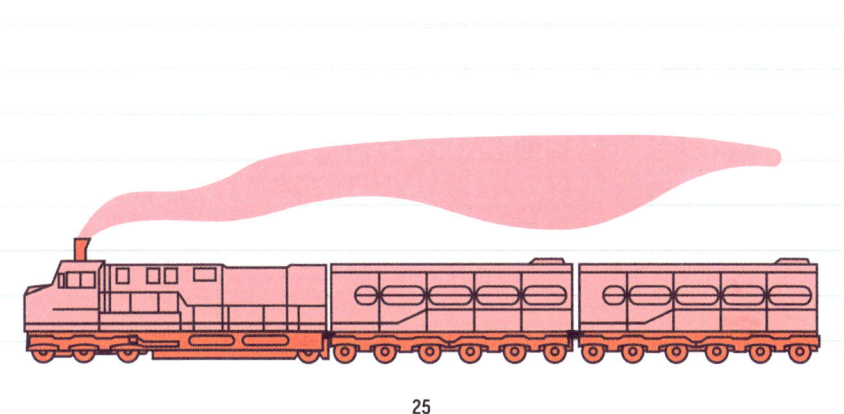

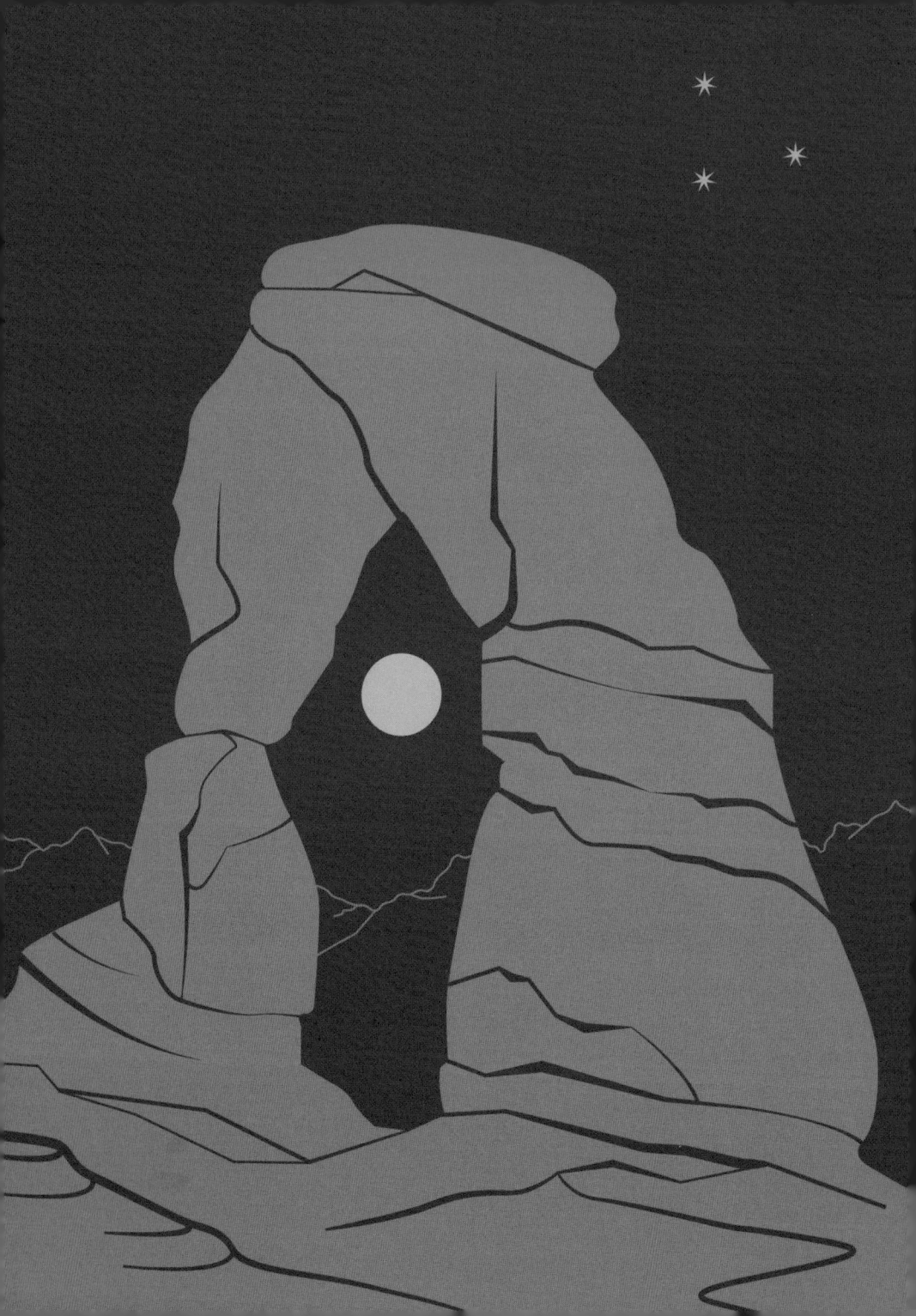

MY ULTIMATE BUCKET LIST

"I haven't been everywhere, but it's on my list."
—Susan Sontag, writer and philosopher

The world is filled with endless experiences, so much so that it can almost feel overwhelming trying to pick what things you absolutely *must do* before you die. Life is short, y'all! To make writing your bucket list a little easier, we've devised some essential categories every traveler should try to tick off. All you need to do is fill in the blanks with the places and things you want to eat, see, and do. Dream big!

EXTRAORDINARY ART

UNUSUAL ARCHITECTURE

UNIQUE FESTIVALS

SPA EXPERIENCES

COLORFUL PLACES

WEIRD MUSEUMS

QUIRKY TOWNS

GIANT THINGS

NATURAL HOT SPRINGS

PLANT PARADISES

ECO-EXPERIENCES

BEAUTIFUL BEACHES

AMAZING ANIMALS

GEOLOGICAL WONDERS

SURREAL SKIES AND VIEWS

EXPERIENCES UP IN THE AIR

UNDERWATER ADVENTURES

HIKES AND TREKS

SPOOKY SPOTS

DAREDEVIL SPORTS

EPIC BARS

FOOD FESTIVALS

EXTRAVAGANT DISHES

MEMORABLE DINING EXPERIENCES

STREET EATS

DECADENT DESSERTS

BOOZE-INFUSED ACTIVITIES

VEGAN & VEGGIE DELIGHTS

Any must-do categories we missed? Add your own below.

THE PLACES I'VE VISITED

Color in all the countries you've been to.

EAT

"First we eat, then we do everything else."
—M. F. K. Fisher, food writer

Is there a better reason to travel than for food? Didn't think so. Aside from fueling our adventures and tasting delicious, food is an incredible way to learn about different cultures, places, and people. When you travel, it can be easy to default to eating things that feel familiar, but if you only eat what you already know, you'll be missing out. Sampling the local cuisine can open you up to a world of different flavors you didn't know existed, so be daring and try as many new things as you can! Who knows? You might even discover your new favorite food.

Food Tip: If authentic food is what you're searching for, look for restaurants filled with locals, not just other tourists. And once you find a spot you like, try asking the staff for their own recommendations of other places to eat. Not only will the food be better, you'll probably save money, too, by avoiding the touristy markups.

BRING ME!
ULTIMATE FOOD BUCKET LIST

From cheap street eats to splurge-worthy meals to unbelievably giant foods, these are dishes everyone should try once in their life.

Jiggle a Perfect, Fluffy Cheesecake in Japan
A light and fluffy soufflé-like cheesecake that is so jiggly you won't be able to resist.
Try it at: Uncle Rikuro's, Osaka

Snack on *Alcapurrias* Beachside in Puerto Rico
This Caribbean snack—a fritter stuffed with ground beef and deep-fried—is best enjoyed on the beach with a cold beer.
Try it at: Any cuchifritos kiosk, or at La Alcapurria Quemá, San Juan

Stuff Your Face with Fresh *Stroopwafel* in the Netherlands
Freshly baked spiced wafers are pressed together with a sweet syrup and then dipped in chocolate for good measure.
Try it at: Rudi's Original Stroopwafels at the Albert Cuyp Market, Amsterdam

Munch on Fried Grasshoppers in Mexico
Chapulines are grasshoppers, but don't be alarmed—the crunchy bugs are delicious when fried and seasoned with chili and lime and served in tortillas with guacamole and salsa.
Try it at: La Casa de Abuela, Oaxaca

Indulge in Lobster Ice Cream in Maine, United States
Vanilla butter–flavored ice cream with cooked lobster folded through, served in a cup or waffle cone. It sounds weird, but it works.
Try it at: Ben & Bills, Bar Harbor, Maine

Have a *Boodle* Fight in the Philippines

A competition-style eating experience where rice, meats, fruits, and vegetables are piled onto a table covered in banana leaves. You eat with your hands, as much as you can, and as fast as possible.

Try it at: Boodle Fight Restaurant & Bar, El Nido, Palawan

Try the Ultimate Multicourse Meal in Morocco

A *diffa* is an epic, multicourse Moroccan feast with appetizers, salads, pastries, soups, barbecued meats, tajine stews, couscous, and platters of sweets.

Try it at: Dar Yacout, Marrakech

Share an Açaí Boat in Brazil

Açaí lovers, join forces to tackle 1.5 gallons (6 liters) of frozen açaí berry purée, topped with fruit, cereal, condensed milk, and chocolate wafers.

Try it at: Açaí Magnífico, São Paulo

Dig Into a Giant Mozzarella Ball in Italy

In a special factory in Italy, you can order a giant ball of mozzarella made from fresh buffalo milk and weighing anywhere from 2.2 to 22 pounds (1kg to 10kg). It's called *La Zizzona* (which means "the big tit"), because it's shaped like a giant breast.

Try it at: La Zizzona di Battipaglia Point, Milano (more locations at www.zizzona.com)

Sample Stinky Tofu in Taiwan

Unofficially known as the "national snack of Taiwan" and found at every good street food stall and night market, fermented tofu is deep-fried and served with pickled cabbage, garlic sauce, and other delicious toppings.

Try it at: Raohe Night Market, Taipei

Order the Wagyu Truffle Cheesesteak in Philadelphia, United States

Philly cheesesteak, but make it *super* fancy—wagyu rib eye, onions, and truffled cheese on a sesame roll, served with a half-bottle of champagne.

Try it at: Barclay Prime, Philadelphia, Pennsylvania

Food Tip: If you have a food allergy and you're traveling to a country where you don't speak the language, write down "I'm allergic to [insert food here]" and ask a local (or Google) to translate it for you into the language of the country you're visiting. Then, anytime you go to a restaurant, you can just whip out your note and show it to the server.

"YOUR BODY IS NOT A TEMPLE, IT'S AN AMUSEMENT PARK. ENJOY THE RIDE."

—Anthony Bourdain, chef

MY FOOD BUCKET LIST

Your turn! Time to create your own food bucket list
so you can record and remember all that delicious grub.

I WANT TO EAT:
Where:

I WANT TO EAT:
Where:

I WANT TO EAT:
Where:

I WANT TO EAT:
Where:

I WANT TO EAT:
Where:

I WANT TO EAT:
Where:

I WANT TO EAT:
Where:

I WANT TO EAT:
Where:

I WANT TO EAT:
Where:

I WANT TO EAT:
Where:

THE BEST THINGS I'VE EVER EATEN

MEMORABLE MEALS

What I ate: ....
Where it was: ....
Why it was so good: ....
....
....
....

What I ate: ....
Where it was: ....
Why it was so good: ....
....
....
....

What I ate: ....
Where it was: ....
Why it was so good: ....
....
....
....

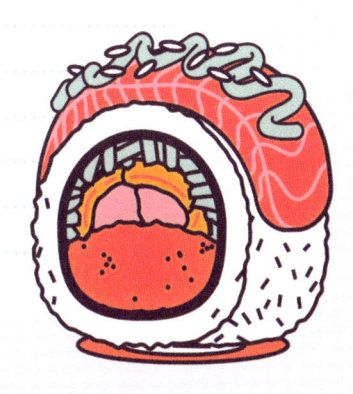

What I ate:

Where it was:

Why it was so good:

What I ate:

Where it was:

Why it was so good:

What I ate:

Where it was:

Why it was so good:

What I ate:

Where it was:

Why it was so good:

TASTY STREET SNACKS

What I ate: ....
Where it was: ....
Why it was so good: ....
....
....
....

What I ate: ....
Where it was: ....
Why it was so good: ....
....
....
....

What I ate: ....
Where it was: ....
Why it was so good: ....
....
....
....

What I ate: ....
Where it was: ....
Why it was so good: ....
....
....
....

What I ate:
Where it was:
Why it was so good:

What I ate:
Where it was:
Why it was so good:

What I ate:
Where it was:
Why it was so good:

Budget Tip: High-end restaurants sometimes offer lunch-only specials that are more affordable, so if there's a fancy spot where you really want to eat, but you're trying to keep your costs down, consider going for a midday meal instead of dinner.

DELICIOUS DRINKS

What I drank: ....
Where it was: ....
Why it was so good: ....
....
....
....

What I drank: ....
Where it was: ....
Why it was so good: ....
....
....
....

What I drank: ....
Where it was: ....
Why it was so good: ....
....
....
....

What I drank: ....
Where it was: ....
Why it was so good: ....
....
....
....

What I drank:
Where it was:
Why it was so good:

What I drank:
Where it was:
Why it was so good:

What I drank:
Where it was:
Why it was so good:

What I drank:
Where it was:
Why it was so good:

DESSERTS AND SWEET TREATS

What I ate: ....
Where it was: ....
Why it was so good: ....

....
....
....

What I ate: ....
Where it was: ....
Why it was so good: ....

....
....
....

What I ate: ....
Where it was: ....
Why it was so good: ....

....
....
....

What I ate: ....
Where it was: ....
Why it was so good: ....

....
....
....

What I ate:
Where it was:
Why it was so good:

What I ate:
Where it was:
Why it was so good:

What I ate:
Where it was:
Why it was so good:

What I ate:
Where it was:
Why it was so good:

ADVENTUROUS EATS

What I ate: ....
Where it was: ....
Why it was so good: ....
....
....
....

What I ate: ....
Where it was: ....
Why it was so good: ....
....
....
....

What I ate: ....
Where it was: ....
Why it was so good: ....
....
....
....

What I ate: ....
Where it was: ....
Why it was so good: ....
....
....
....

What I ate:
Where it was:
Why it was so good:

What I ate:
Where it was:
Why it was so good:

What I ate:
Where it was:
Why it was so good:

What I ate:
Where it was:
Why it was so good:

RANDOM BITES

What I ate: ....

Where it was: ....

Why it was so good: ....

....

....

....

What I ate: ....

Where it was: ....

Why it was so good: ....

....

....

....

What I ate: ....

Where it was: ....

Why it was so good: ....

....

....

....

What I ate: ....

Where it was: ....

Why it was so good: ....

....

....

....

What I ate:

Where it was:

Why it was so good:

What I ate:

Where it was:

Why it was so good:

What I ate:

Where it was:

Why it was so good:

If you're a visual eater, doodle your favorite dishes and food experiences below:

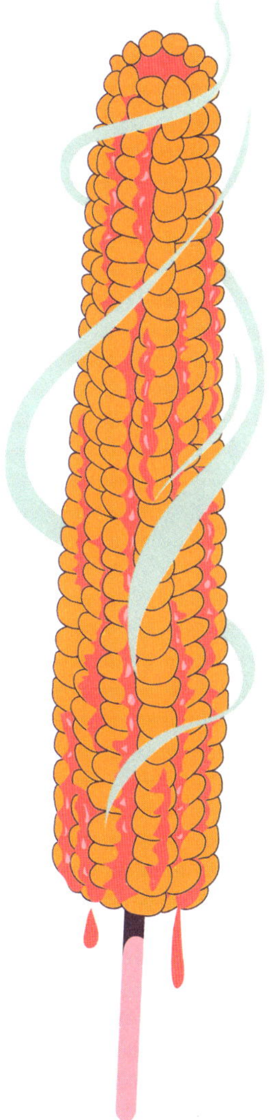

SEE

"A traveler without observation is a bird without wings."
—Saadi Shirazi, poet

If there's ever a time to open our eyes and take in the world around us, it's when we travel—to see how other people live, to learn, to broaden our perspectives, and to forge incredible memories to take home with us. We learn about other cultures via their art, architecture, and sometimes just by sitting outside and people watching. And we find new appreciation for the natural world and all its wonders when we put down our cameras and just experience nature in all its glory. The sunsets are never quite the same in photos!

> **Travel Tip:** If you follow the crowds, you'll usually find something worth checking out; things are popular for a reason! But take the time to ask around for other recommendations, and you might discover there's a better view just around the corner that only the locals know about.

BRING ME!
ULTIMATE SEE LIST

So many amazing things to see, so little time. Colorful villages, vivid natural wonders, unusual museums, art, architecture, and adorable animals. Here are a few sights that deserve a spot on your bucket list.

Discover the Colorful Street Art in Valparaíso, Chile

The local government encourages street art in this vibrant city, where you'll find an abundance of giant murals, outdoor paintings, and amazing mosaics.

See it at: There are surprises to find all over the city's streets, but start at Concepción Hill and the open-air museum of Bellavista Hill

See the Upside-Down Baobab Trees in Madagascar

There's a stretch of road in Madagascar called Avenue of the Baobabs where you can see surreal-looking, 800-year-old trees that appear to have been planted upside down.

See it at: The dirt road that runs between Andriamena and Marofototra in Madagascar's Menabe region

Dive into Stunning Blue Holes in the Bahamas

The Blue Holes comprise an underwater cave system that is striking to see from above—deep blue circles surrounded by lighter turquoise waters. You can dive into the caves, or swim/snorkel in shallow waters around the entrance to the holes.

See it at: Andros Island in the Bahamas

Visit the Great Mosque in Mali

This is the largest mud-built structure in the world and a marvel of religious architecture. The mosque you can see today is a reconstruction of the original (which was built in the thirteenth or fourteenth century), and, due to the region's harsh climate, there's a festival every year where everyone gathers to slather more mud over it.

See it at: Djenné, Mali

Walk along The Red Beach in China

This wetland ecosystem is covered in aquatic plants that carpet the water in vivid red in the fall. So it's not actually a beach, but paired with the neighboring green rice paddies, it's an incredible, colorful sight.

See it at: The Liaohe River Delta, near Panjin City in Liaoning Province, China

Wander the Nubian Villages in Egypt

The Nubian Villages near Aswan are famous for their richly decorated, brightly colored, curved mud-brick houses. The villages are home to Nubian peoples, an ethno-linguistic group indigenous to northern Sudan and southern Egypt.

See it at: Elephantine Island, near the city of Aswan, Egypt

Spend a While in a Cup Noodles Museum in Japan

Instant ramen lovers: This museum is dedicated to all things instant noodles and Cup Noodles, along with exhibits honoring the Taiwanese-Japanese inventor of Cup Noodles, Momofuku Ando. Most iconic is the instant noodles tunnel, with walls covered in 800 kinds of noodles packaging.

See it at: One of two locations in Yokohama or Ikeda, Osaka

Be Dazzled at Medellín Flower Fair in Colombia

This floral extravaganza happens every August in Medellín, the "city of eternal spring." A lot goes on during the festival, but make sure you see the parade of the *silleteros* (flower vendors), where growers attach giant circular flower arrangements to their backs and parade them through the city to cheering crowds.

See it at: Medellín, Antioquia, Colombia

Stroll an Endless Art Park in Russia

Nikola-Lenivets is a sprawling art park with dozens of landscape installations and other outdoor art objects from Russian and international artists. It's also where you can find Russia's answer to Burning Man—Archstoyanie—if that's your thing.

See it at: Ugra National Park, Kaluga Oblast, Russia

Admire Beluga Whales in Canada

Called the "canaries of the sea," beluga whales are adorable creatures with high-pitched chirps, and you can see—or swim among—them in Canada. Do your research to make sure you're going with an ethical tour company. The whales are friendly and can be injured if the boats they swim close to aren't equipped with proper guards.

See it at: Churchill River in Manitoba, Canada

Gaze Up at the Northern Lights in Iceland

Iceland is just one of many places to see the northern lights, or aurora borealis. You can go on an aurora-hunting guided tour, take a northern lights cruise, or, with a bit of planning (and luck!), see the magical sky show by yourself.

See it at: It's possible to see the aurora borealis all over Iceland in areas with little light pollution, but it can sometimes also be seen from the city of Reykjavík, too.

Travel Tip: It can take a bit of patience to see the northern lights—the sky needs to be clear and dark enough and the sun needs to be in a plasma-emitting cycle. The best time of year to visit is between late August and mid-April. It's best to spend a bit longer in your destination (ideally, more than seven to ten days) to maximize your chances of seeing the light show. If you do book a guided tour, book it close to the beginning of your trip; if the weather is bad, there is time to reschedule and often tours will offer a free retry.

"ONE'S DESTINATION IS NEVER A PLACE, BUT A NEW WAY OF SEEING THINGS."

—Henry Miller, writer and artist

MY SEE BUCKET LIST

Your turn! Record all the cool, interesting, unique things you've seen on your trip.

I WANT TO SEE:
Where:

I WANT TO SEE:
Where:

I WANT TO SEE:
Where:

I WANT TO SEE:
Where:

I WANT TO SEE:
Where:

I WANT TO SEE:
Where:

I WANT TO SEE:
Where:

I WANT TO SEE:
Where:

I WANT TO SEE:
Where:

I WANT TO SEE:
Where:

THE BEST THINGS I'VE EVER SEEN

NATURAL WONDERS

What I saw: ....
Where it was: ....
Why it was so good: ....
....
....
....

What I saw: ....
Where it was: ....
Why it was so good: ....
....
....
....

What I saw: ....
Where it was: ....
Why it was so good: ....
....
....
....

What I saw:
Where it was:
Why it was so good:

What I saw:
Where it was:
Why it was so good:

What I saw:
Where it was:
Why it was so good:

What I saw:
Where it was:
Why it was so good:

CITY SIGHTS

What I saw: ....
Where it was: ....
Why it was so good: ....
....
....
....

What I saw: ....
Where it was: ....
Why it was so good: ....
....
....
....

What I saw: ....
Where it was: ....
Why it was so good: ....
....
....
....

What I saw: ....
Where it was: ....
Why it was so good: ....
....
....
....

What I saw:
Where it was:
Why it was so good:

What I saw:
Where it was:
Why it was so good:

What I saw:
Where it was:
Why it was so good:

What I saw:
Where it was:
Why it was so good:

COLORFUL PLACES

What I saw: ....
Where it was: ....
Why it was so good: ....
....
....
....

What I saw: ....
Where it was: ....
Why it was so good: ....
....
....
....

What I saw: ....
Where it was: ....
Why it was so good: ....
....
....
....

What I saw: ....
Where it was: ....
Why it was so good: ....
....
....
....

What I saw:
Where it was:
Why it was so good:

What I saw:
Where it was:
Why it was so good:

What I saw:
Where it was:
Why it was so good:

SCENIC SPOTS

What I saw: ....
Where it was: ....
Why it was so good: ....
....
....
....

What I saw: ....
Where it was: ....
Why it was so good: ....
....
....
....

What I saw: ....
Where it was: ....
Why it was so good: ....
....
....
....

What I saw: ....
Where it was: ....
Why it was so good: ....
....
....
....

What I saw:

Where it was:

Why it was so good:

What I saw:

Where it was:

Why it was so good:

What I saw:

Where it was:

Why it was so good:

> "Stuff your eyes with wonder, live as if you'd drop dead in ten seconds. See the world. It's more fantastic than any dream made or paid for in factories."
>
> —Ray Bradbury, author and screenwriter

AMAZING WILDLIFE

What I saw:
Where it was:
Why it was so good:

What I saw:
Where it was:
Why it was so good:

What I saw:
Where it was:
Why it was so good:

What I saw:
Where it was:
Why it was so good:

What I saw:
Where it was:
Why it was so good:

What I saw:
Where it was:
Why it was so good:

What I saw:
Where it was:
Why it was so good:

What I saw:
Where it was:
Why it was so good:

ART AND ARCHITECTURE

What I saw: ....
Where it was: ....
Why it was so good: ....
....
....
....

What I saw: ....
Where it was: ....
Why it was so good: ....
....
....
....

What I saw: ....
Where it was: ....
Why it was so good: ....
....
....
....

What I saw: ....
Where it was: ....
Why it was so good: ....
....
....
....

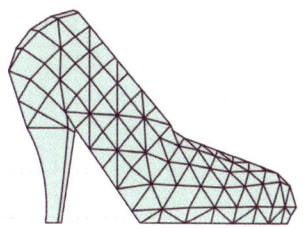

What I saw:
Where it was:
Why it was so good:

What I saw:
Where it was:
Why it was so good:

What I saw:
Where it was:
Why it was so good:

What I saw:
Where it was:
Why it was so good:

MEMORABLE VIEWS

What I saw: ....
Where it was: ....
Why it was so good: ....
....
....
....

What I saw: ....
Where it was: ....
Why it was so good: ....
....
....
....

What I saw: ....
Where it was: ....
Why it was so good: ....
....
....

What I saw: ....
Where it was: ....
Why it was so good: ....
....
....
....

What I saw:
Where it was:
Why it was so good:

What I saw:
Where it was:
Why it was so good:

What I saw:
Where it was:
Why it was so good:

What I saw:
Where it was:
Why it was so good:

Finding it hard to describe something you saw with words? Draw it here!

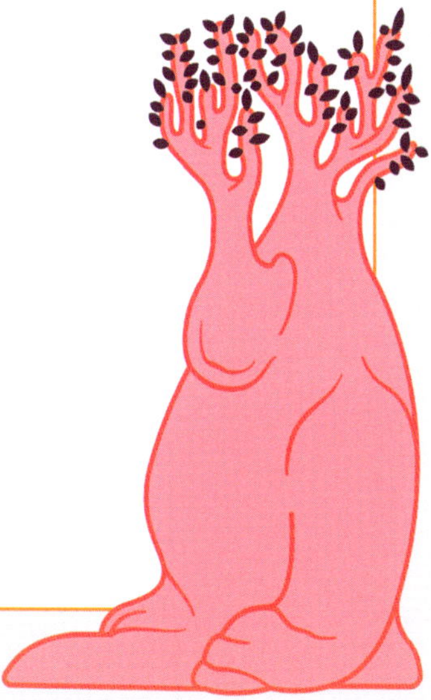

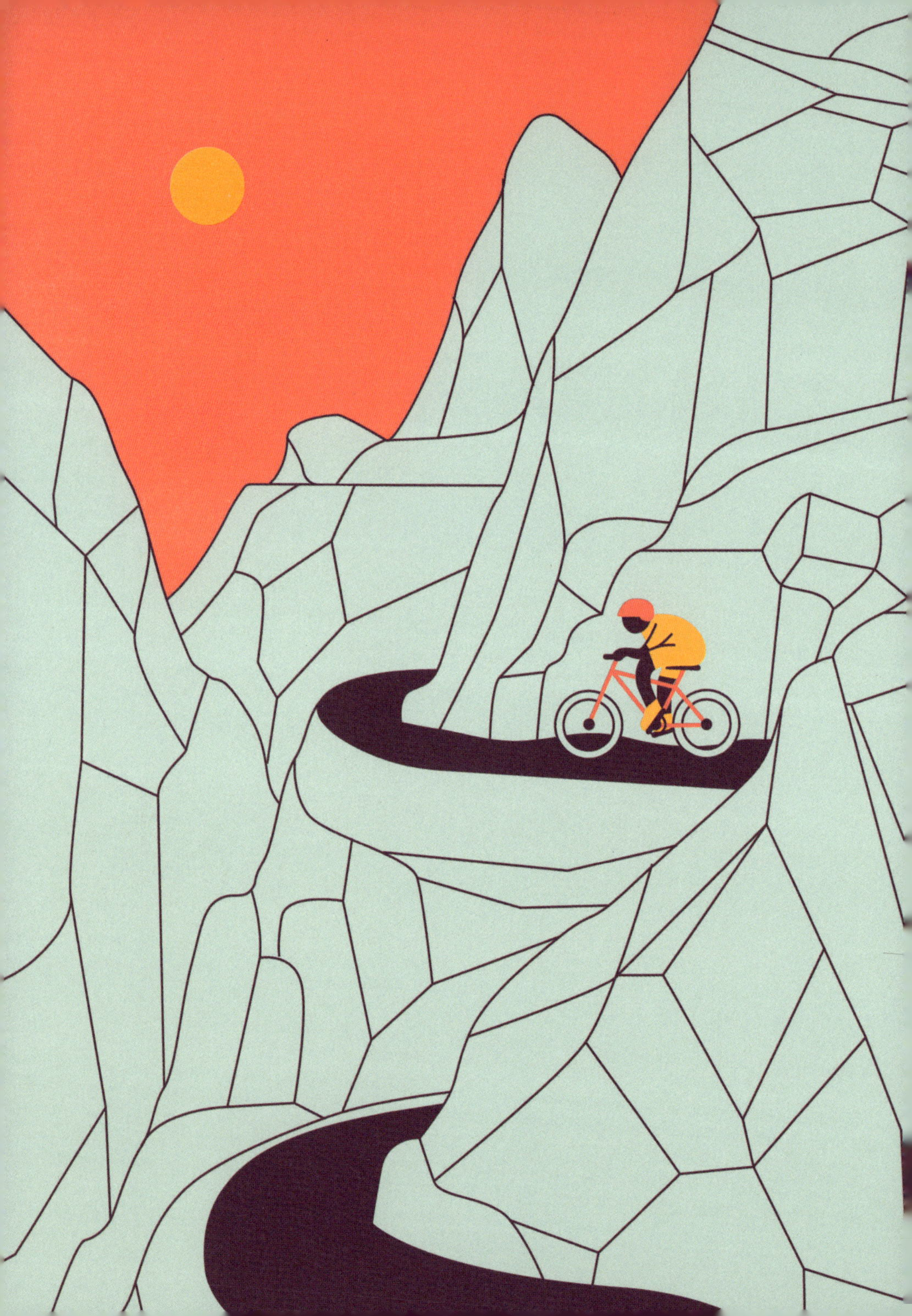

DO

"Twenty years from now you will be more disappointed by the things you didn't do than by the ones you did. So throw off the bowlines, sail away from the safe harbor. Catch the trade winds in your sails. Explore. Dream."

—Mark Twain, writer and humorist

To paraphrase Mr. Twain, you're far more likely to regret the things you didn't do than the things you did. The world is massive and full of opportunities, especially for keen, curious, and adventurous travelers. Traveling can be daunting and scary at times, but that's also what makes it exciting and why it helps us grow (surely you've heard that cliché about how the magic happens when you step out of your comfort zone). So when you're ready, muster the courage to embrace the unknown and discover all the awesome things to do, both near and far. And then, don't just *think* about doing them—make a plan and actually do them. Use your common sense, trust your gut, and keep your values in mind and you can't go wrong. Let's go!

BRING ME!
ULTIMATE DO LIST

Exploring geological wonders, cage-diving with crocs, go-karting through city streets . . . here are just a few of our favorite thrilling, unique, and fascinating experiences we think you owe it to yourself to do.

Fly in a Hot-Air Balloon over Fairy Chimneys in Turkey
Carved by wind and rain over millions of years, there's no better way to experience the magical landscape of Cappadocia than by taking flight in a hot-air balloon at sunrise.
Where to go: The nearby town of Göreme, where many tour companies offer hot-air balloon rides

Sleep in a 1,200-Foot-High Suspended Lodge in Peru
Climb up the side of a mountain to reach your bed in a private, transparent capsule that offers epic views of the Sacred Valley below. Then in the morning, zip-line back to solid ground.
Where to go: Skylodge Adventure Suites in Cusco

Wind through the Rocky Mountains in a Glass-Roofed Train in Canada
The Rocky Mountaineer is a luxury train experience that runs through the stunning Canadian Rockies, and, thanks to its glass-domed ceiling, you get *all* the views. Oh, and it doesn't hurt that the food is incredible.
Where to go: The First Passage to the West route on the Rocky Mountaineer, departing in Vancouver

Hike along a Sandstone Wave in Arizona, United States

Located in the north of Arizona just over the border from Utah, this spectacular rock formation looks like a natural half-pipe, rippled with lines of pink, orange, red, and white Navajo sandstone. A six-mile hike will take you there—if you can score a coveted permit.

Where to go: The Wave in Coyote Buttes North, Arizona

Go Hot-Springs Hopping in the Azores, Portugal

The Azorean island of São Miguel is a hot-springs haven, thanks to its volcanic origins, so it's the perfect place to go on your own self-guided natural spa tour. Don't miss Ponta da Ferraria, a magical hot spring that feeds directly into the Atlantic Ocean.

Where to go: São Miguel Island in the Azores

Walk on the Wing of an Airplane in England

For the ultimate daredevil experience, you can't beat wing-walking on a classic 1940s biplane as it cruises through the sky or performs dips and dives at speeds of up to 140 miles per hour.

Where to go: Gloucestershire, with the team of professional wing-walkers at AeroSuperBatics

Trek with Gorillas in Rwanda

Not only is the opportunity to witness these marvelous animals in their natural habitat totally bucket list–worthy, but gorilla trekking also brings significant income to local communities and helps contribute to conservation efforts.

Where to go: Volcanoes National Park in northwest Rwanda

Kayak through a Glow-in-the-Dark Bay in Puerto Rico

Mosquito Bay holds the title of the brightest bioluminescent bay in the world, according to the folks at Guinness World Records. And the best way to experience it is in a clear-bottomed kayak: the microscopic organisms glow a neon-blue when disturbed (by things like your paddle!), making the water look like it's shimmering with shining stars.

Where to go: Mosquito Bay on Vieques, Puerto Rico

Ride above Forests on a Pedal-Powered Zip Line in the Philippines

On the island of Bohol in the Philippines, you can cycle 150 feet (45 meters) in the air on a pedal-powered zip line. Go it alone or grab your buddy and make it a race. Either way, be sure to soak up the epic views of the surrounding Chocolate Hills.

Where to go: Chocolate Hills Adventure Park in Bohol

Cage Dive with Saltwater Crocodiles in Australia

This spine-tingling experience at Crocosaurus Cove in Australia's Northern Territory lets you come snout-to-snout with a 16-foot saltwater crocodile, all from the safety of a acryllic-glass cage, provided you're not scared off by the experience's name, Cage of Death.

Where to go: Crocosaurus Cove in Darwin, Australia

Drive Go-Karts through City Streets in Japan

Forget hop-on, hop-off buses: Dress up in costume and zip through the streets of Tokyo on what might just be the most unique sightseeing experience ever.

Where to go: Street Kart in Tokyo, Japan

Travel Tip: While it can be helpful to have an idea of the things you really want to do, overplanning can be the enemy of a great trip. Make sure you allow for time to "do nothing" and be spontaneous—sometimes the best adventures happen on the spur of the moment.

MY DO BUCKET LIST

Your turn! Use this space to plan for—and record—
all the cool things you want to do on your trip.

I WANT TO:
Where:

I WANT TO:
Where:

I WANT TO:
Where:

I WANT TO:
Where:

I WANT TO:
Where:

I WANT TO:
Where:

I WANT TO:
Where:

I WANT TO:
Where:

I WANT TO:
Where:

I WANT TO:
Where:

"If you think adventure is dangerous,
try routine; it is lethal."

—Paulo Coelho, lyricist and novelist

THE BEST THINGS I'VE EVER DONE

EXTREME ACTIVITIES

What I did: ....
Where it was: ....
Why it was so good: ....
....
....
....

What I did: ....
Where it was: ....
Why it was so good: ....
....
....
....

What I did: ....
Where it was: ....
Why it was so good: ....
....
....
....

What I did:
Where it was:
Why it was so good:

What I did:
Where it was:
Why it was so good:

What I did:
Where it was:
Why it was so good:

What I did:
Where it was:
Why it was so good:

THRILLING PLACES

What I did:
Where it was:
Why it was so good:

What I did:
Where it was:
Why it was so good:

What I did:
Where it was:
Why it was so good:

What I did:
Where it was:
Why it was so good:

What I did:
Where it was:
Why it was so good:

What I did:
Where it was:
Why it was so good:

What I did:
Where it was:
Why it was so good:

What I did:
Where it was:
Why it was so good:

HIKES AND TREKS

What I did: ....
Where it was: ....
Why it was so good: ....
....
....
....

What I did: ....
Where it was: ....
Why it was so good: ....
....
....
....

What I did: ....
Where it was: ....
Why it was so good: ....
....
....
....

What I did: ....
Where it was: ....
Why it was so good: ....
....
....
....

What I did:
Where it was:
Why it was so good:

What I did:
Where it was:
Why it was so good:

What I did:
Where it was:
Why it was so good:

Hiking Tip: Before you set out on any hike, always tell a friend or family member exactly where you're going and when you'll be back. You can also record your location and plans as your voicemail greeting so if people try to call but can't reach you, they'll hear where you're supposed to be.

COOL FESTIVALS

What I did: ....
Where it was: ....
Why it was so good: ....

....
....
....

What I did: ....
Where it was: ....
Why it was so good: ....

....
....
....

What I did: ....
Where it was: ....
Why it was so good: ....

....
....
....

What I did: ....
Where it was: ....
Why it was so good: ....

....
....
....

What I did:

Where it was:

Why it was so good:

What I did:

Where it was:

Why it was so good:

What I did:

Where it was:

Why it was so good:

QUIRKY MUSEUMS

What I did: ....
Where it was: ....
Why it was so good: ....
....
....
....

What I did: ....
Where it was: ....
Why it was so good: ....
....
....
....

What I did: ....
Where it was: ....
Why it was so good: ....
....
....
....

What I did: ....
Where it was: ....
Why it was so good: ....
....
....
....

What I did:

Where it was:

Why it was so good:

What I did:

Where it was:

Why it was so good:

What I did:

Where it was:

Why it was so good:

What I did:

Where it was:

Why it was so good:

WILD RIDES

What I did: ....
Where it was: ....
Why it was so good: ....
....
....
....

What I did: ....
Where it was: ....
Why it was so good: ....
....
....
....

What I did: ....
Where it was: ....
Why it was so good: ....
....
....
....

What I did: ....
Where it was: ....
Why it was so good: ....
....
....
....

What I did:
Where it was:
Why it was so good:

What I did:
Where it was:
Why it was so good:

What I did:
Where it was:
Why it was so good:

What I did:
Where it was:
Why it was so good:

If words can't quite capture all that you did, draw your adventures below:

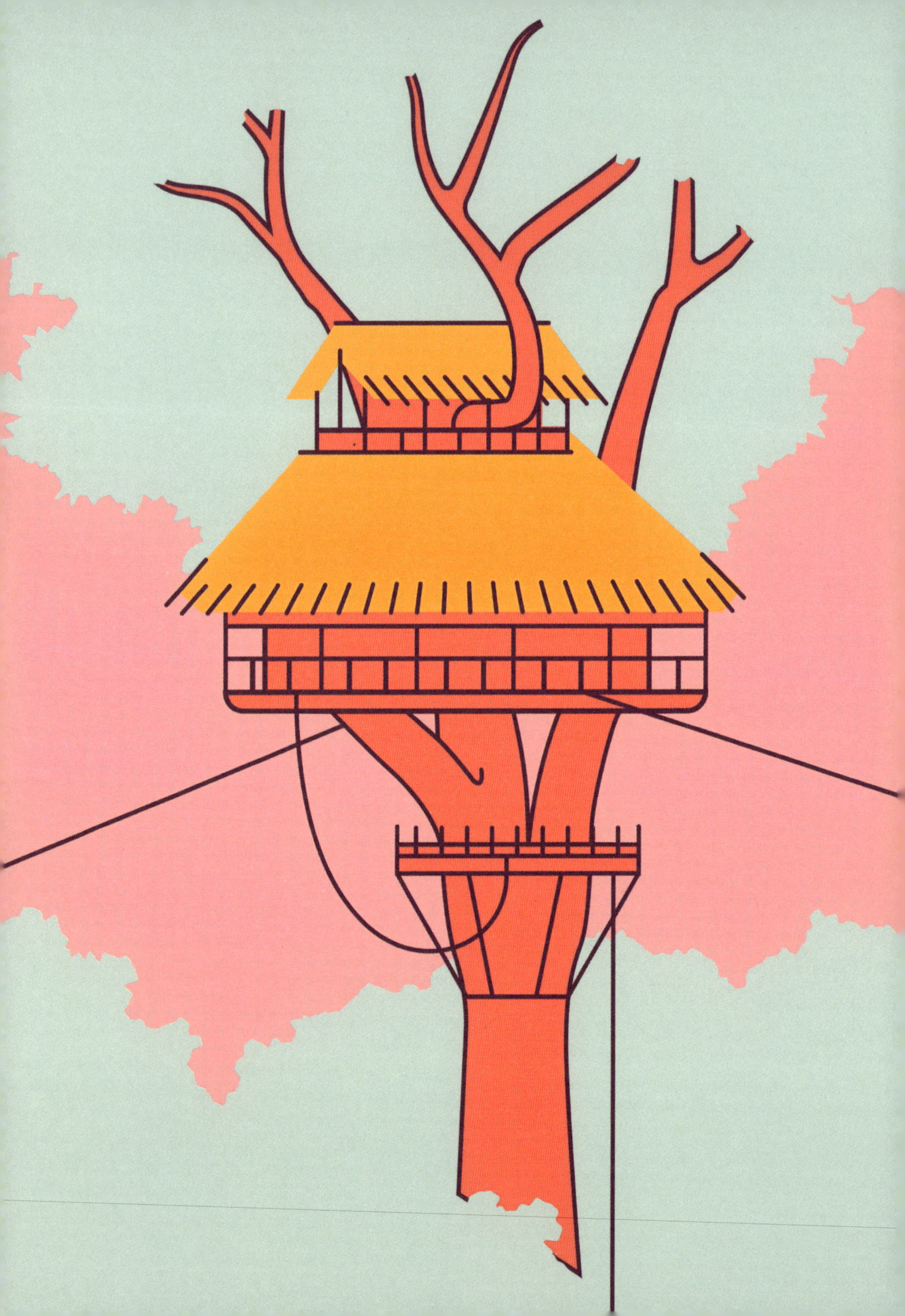

MEET

"A journey is best measured in friends, rather than miles."
—Tim Cahill, travel writer

Just like the places you see and the things you do, the people you encounter along the way make your trip that much more special. So regardless of whether you're exploring solo or traveling in a group, be curious, be kind, and be interested. Get to know the locals, your fellow travelers, even new furry (and scaly and feathery) friends—because most experiences are better when they're shared.

ICE BREAKERS

When you've had enough of talking about the weather, get the conversation flowing with these games, questions, and prompts.

> ### WHERE DO YOU STAND ON THESE POLARIZING TRAVEL OPINIONS?

Suitcase or **backpack**?

Check-in luggage or **carry-on only**?

Overpack or **underpack**?

Airbnb or **hotel**?

Window seat or **aisle seat**?

Talk to your seat neighbor or **keep to yourself**?

Jam-packed itinerary or **figure it out as you go**?

Travel solo or **with a big group of people**?

Hotel turndown service or **do not disturb**?

Fine dining or **street food**?

Beach or **snow**?

Small town or **big city**?

Travel by train or **by car**?

Splurge on one big trip or **take lots of small trips**?

Spend a long time in one destination or **a short time in many destinations**?

THE HARDEST "WOULD YOU RATHER" QUESTIONS FOR TRAVELERS

Would you rather . . .

. . . relax at an all-inclusive resort in Cancun or go on a three-day hike in Patagonia?

. . . swim with pigs in the Bahamas or trek with gorillas in Rwanda?

. . . see every piece of art at the Louvre or go on every ride at Disneyland?

. . . sleep in a jungle treehouse in Costa Rica or in an underwater hotel in the Maldives?

. . . eat pasta in Rome or ramen in Tokyo?

. . . see the northern lights in Iceland or witness the Great Wildebeest Migration in Kenya?

. . . ride the world's fastest roller coaster in Abu Dhabi or zip-line across the rain forest in Puerto Rico?

. . . snorkel in the Great Barrier Reef in Australia or swim with sea turtles in the Galápagos Islands in Ecuador?

TRAVEL TRIVIA QUESTIONS

1. What is the capital of Tanzania?

2. Where are the Pyrenees?

3. A quokka is native to which country?

4. How many countries start with the letter "I"?
   (Bonus points if you can name them all.)

5. What is the second-largest city in the world, by population?

6. Which Canadian animal is known as a "sea canary"?

7. What is injera?

8. How do you say *cheers* in German?

9. What is the currency of Serbia?

10. How long is the flight from Los Angeles to Tokyo?

11. Where will you find the world's tallest building?

12. If you're in Oaxaca, which country are you in?

> "We travel, some of us forever, to seek other places, other lives, other souls."
>
> —Anaïs Nin, author

13. What is the national dish of Vietnam?

14. Which country has the most rain-forest coverage?

15. What colors are on the South Korean flag?

16. How many countries share a border with Slovakia? (Bonus points if you can name them all.)

17. Which country has the longest total coastline?

18. Where is the oldest tree in the world?

19. True or false: Sweden has more islands than any other country.

20. In Australian slang, what does the term "budgie smugglers" refer to?

Travel Trivia Answers

1. Dodoma **2.** Border of Spain and France **3.** Eight (Iceland, India, Indonesia, Iran, Iraq, Ireland, Israel, Italy) **5.** Delhi, India **6.** Beluga whale **7.** A spongy, sourdough flatbread commonly eaten in Ethiopia and Eritrea **8.** "Prost!" **9.** Serbian dinar **10.** Approximately 11 hours **11.** Burj Khalifa in Dubai **12.** Pho **13.** Mexico **14.** Brazil **15.** Red, blue, black, white **16.** Five (Austria, Czechia, Hungary, Poland, Ukraine) **17.** Canada **18.** California, United States (Great Basin Bristlecone Pine) **19.** True **20.** Tight-fitting swimming briefs

PEOPLE TO REMEMBER

NAME: .... **@:** ....

EMAIL: .... **PHONE:** ....

WHERE WE MET: ....

MEMORABLE MOMENT: ....

....

NAME: .... **@:** ....

EMAIL: .... **PHONE:** ....

WHERE WE MET: ....

MEMORABLE MOMENT: ....

....

NAME: .... **@:** ....

EMAIL: .... **PHONE:** ....

WHERE WE MET: ....

MEMORABLE MOMENT: ....

....

NAME: .... **@:** ....

EMAIL: .... **PHONE:** ....

WHERE WE MET: ....

MEMORABLE MOMENT: ....

....

NAME: **@:**
EMAIL: **PHONE:**
WHERE WE MET:
MEMORABLE MOMENT:

NAME: **@:**
EMAIL: **PHONE:**
WHERE WE MET:
MEMORABLE MOMENT:

NAME: **@:**
EMAIL: **PHONE:**
WHERE WE MET:
MEMORABLE MOMENT:

NAME: **@:**
EMAIL: **PHONE:**
WHERE WE MET:
MEMORABLE MOMENT:

PEOPLE TO REMEMBER

NAME: .... @: ....
EMAIL: .... PHONE: ....
WHERE WE MET: ....
MEMORABLE MOMENT: ....
....

NAME: .... @: ....
EMAIL: .... PHONE: ....
WHERE WE MET: ....
MEMORABLE MOMENT: ....
....

NAME: .... @: ....
EMAIL: .... PHONE: ....
WHERE WE MET: ....
MEMORABLE MOMENT: ....
....

NAME: .... @: ....
EMAIL: .... PHONE: ....
WHERE WE MET: ....
MEMORABLE MOMENT: ....
....

NAME: @:
EMAIL: PHONE:
WHERE WE MET:
MEMORABLE MOMENT:

NAME: @:
EMAIL: PHONE:
WHERE WE MET:
MEMORABLE MOMENT:

NAME: @:
EMAIL: PHONE:
WHERE WE MET:
MEMORABLE MOMENT:

"The more I traveled the more I realized that fear makes strangers of people who should be friends."

—Shirley MacLaine, actor

Use this space to stick photos, jot down thoughts, or sketch the friends you meet along the way.

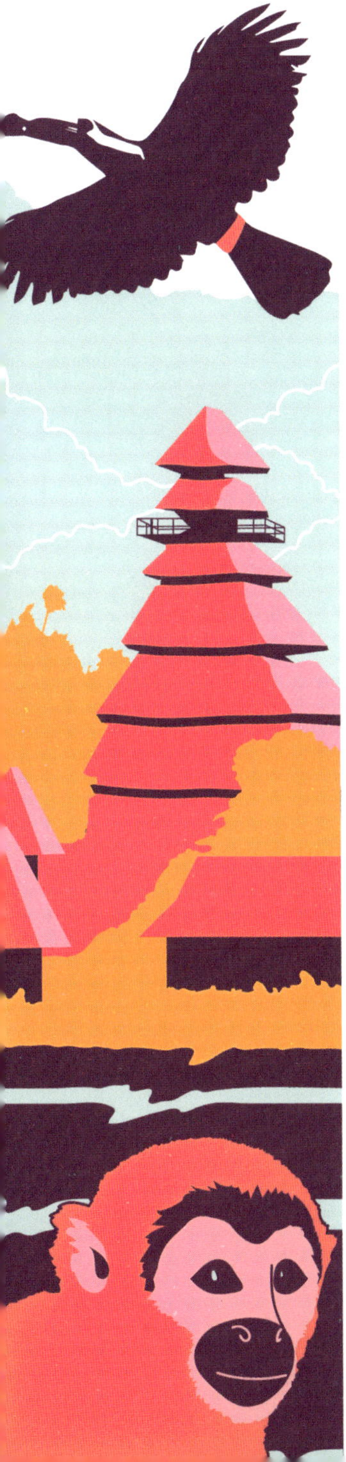

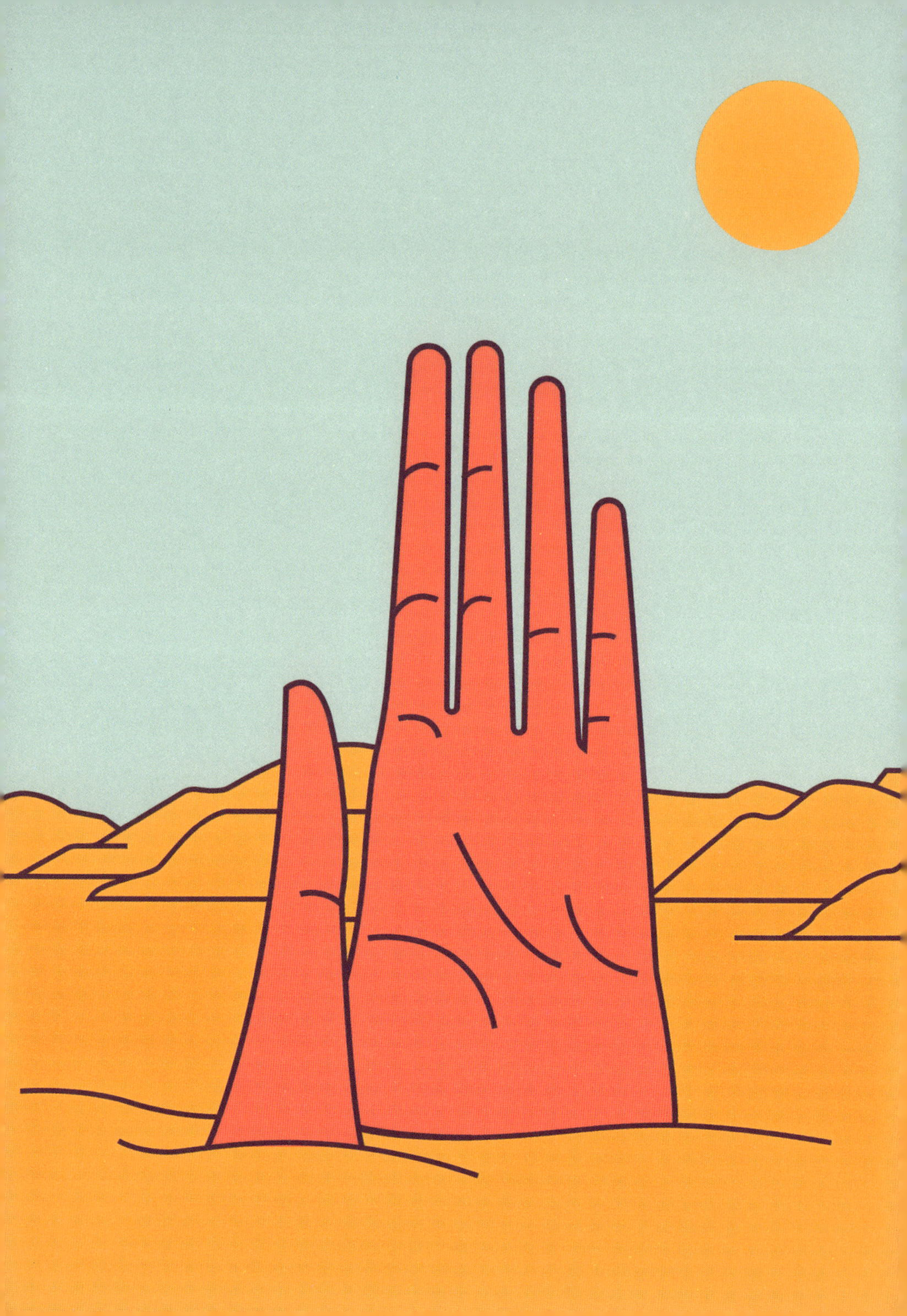

TRIP PLANNING AND REFLECTIONS

"I never travel without my diary. One should always have something sensational to read in the train."

—Oscar Wilde, poet and playwright

TRIP PLANNER

Trip Name: ....
Where: ....
When: ....
With Whom: ....
Weather: ....

My Itinerary: ....

PACKING LIST

The Basic Stuff

- Travel docs
- This journal
- Reading material
- Travel pillow
- Sleeping mask
- Headphones
- Earplugs
- Phone charger
- Pen
- Eyeglasses
- Travel lock
- Snacks
- Chewing gum
- Universal adaptor
- Reusable straw
- Reusable water bottle
- Debit card and backup debit card
- Emergency cash
- Other ....

Stuff to Wear

- Underwear
- Socks
- Bottoms
- Tops
- Sweaters
- Dresses and pants
- Waterproof jacket
- Swimsuit
- Jacket
- Watch
- Flip-flops
- Sneakers
- Hiking boots
- Casual shoes
- Hat
- Sunglasses
- Gloves
- Workout clothes
- Belt
- Other ....

Toiletries and Health-Related Items

Medications
Hand sanitizer
First aid kit
Toothbrush, toothpaste, dental floss
Mouthwash
Hairbrush/comb
Insect repellant
Period products
Vitamins
Cotton swabs
Tissues
Sunscreen and after-sun lotion
Baby wipes
Tweezers
Body wash
Contact lenses and saline solution
Shampoo and conditioner
Shaving stuff
Other

Little Extras

Mini lint roller
Laundry pen/stain remover
Portable battery pack
Flashlight
Umbrella
Mini sewing kit
Other

REFLECTIONS

Why I picked this trip:

When I set off on my trip I felt:

The places I went looked like:

The places I went smelled like:

The best thing(s) I ate:

The best thing(s) I saw:

The best thing(s) I did:

The best place(s) I went:

Things I experienced for the first time:

Things that surprised me:

Things that inspired me:

Things that challenged me:

Things that made me laugh:

The most exciting part of my trip:

I really appreciated it when:

I felt the happiest when:

One thing I did that I wasn't planning on doing:

One thing I did that was way better than I expected:

Some important things I learned:

Souvenirs I bought on my trip:

The most interesting people I met:

One thing that put me out of my comfort zone:

One thing that reminded me of home:

This trip made me grateful for:

How I felt about leaving:

What I discovered about myself:

What I'd do differently if I could take this trip again:

How this trip changed me for the better:

Other notes:

TRIP PLANNER

Trip Name: ....
Where: ....
When: ....
With Whom: ....
Weather: ....

My Itinerary: ....

....
....
....
....
....
....
....
....
....
....
....
....
....
....
....
....
....
....
....
....

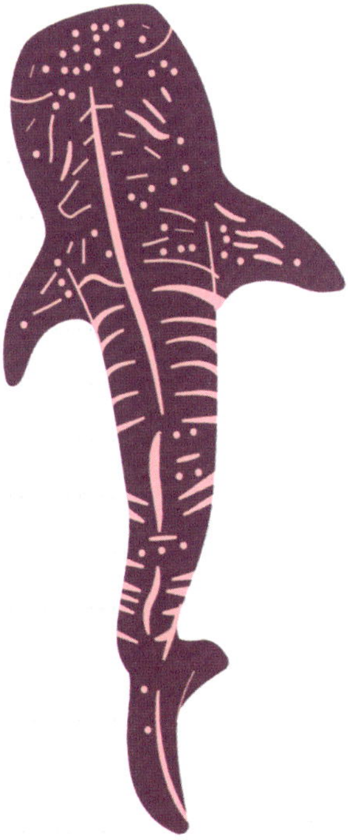

PACKING LIST

The Basic Stuff

- Travel docs
- This journal
- Reading material
- Travel pillow
- Sleeping mask
- Headphones
- Earplugs
- Phone charger
- Pen
- Eyeglasses
- Travel lock
- Snacks
- Chewing gum
- Universal adaptor
- Reusable straw
- Reusable water bottle
- Debit card and backup debit card
- Emergency cash
- Other ....

Stuff to Wear

- Underwear
- Socks
- Bottoms
- Tops
- Sweaters
- Dresses and pants
- Waterproof jacket
- Swimsuit
- Jacket
- Watch
- Flip-flops
- Sneakers
- Hiking boots
- Casual shoes
- Hat
- Sunglasses
- Gloves
- Workout clothes
- Belt
- Other ....

Toiletries and Health-Related Items

Medications
Hand sanitizer
First aid kit
Toothbrush, toothpaste, dental floss
Mouthwash
Hairbrush/comb
Insect repellant
Period products
Vitamins
Cotton swabs
Tissues
Sunscreen and after-sun lotion
Baby wipes
Tweezers
Body wash
Contact lenses and saline solution
Shampoo and conditioner
Shaving stuff
Other

Little Extras

Mini lint roller
Laundry pen/stain remover
Portable battery pack
Flashlight
Umbrella
Mini sewing kit
Other

REFLECTIONS

Why I picked this trip:

When I set off on my trip I felt:

The places I went looked like:

The places I went smelled like:

The best thing(s) I ate:

The best thing(s) I saw:

The best thing(s) I did:

The best place(s) I went:

Things I experienced for the first time:

Things that surprised me:

Things that inspired me:

Things that challenged me:

Things that made me laugh:

The most exciting part of my trip:

I really appreciated it when:

I felt the happiest when:

One thing I did that I wasn't planning on doing:

One thing I did that was way better than I expected:

Some important things I learned:

Souvenirs I bought on my trip:

The most interesting people I met:

One thing that put me out of my comfort zone:

One thing that reminded me of home:

This trip made me grateful for:

How I felt about leaving:

What I discovered about myself:

What I'd do differently if I could take this trip again:

How this trip changed me for the better:

Other notes:

TRIP PLANNER

Trip Name: ....

Where: ....

When: ....

With Whom: ....

Weather: ....

My Itinerary: ....

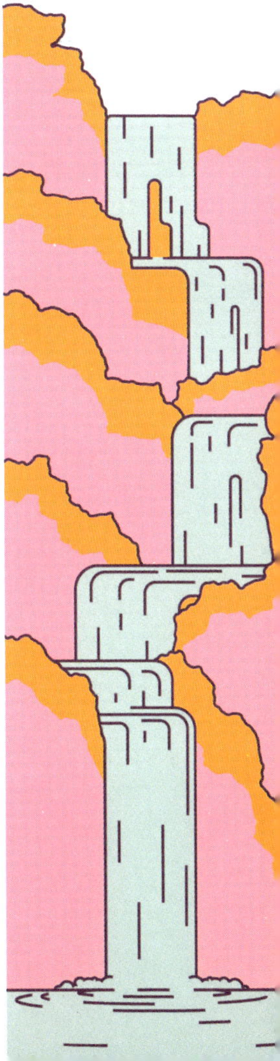

PACKING LIST

The Basic Stuff

- Travel docs
- This journal
- Reading material
- Travel pillow
- Sleeping mask
- Headphones
- Earplugs
- Phone charger
- Pen
- Eyeglasses
- Travel lock
- Snacks
- Chewing gum
- Universal adaptor
- Reusable straw
- Reusable water bottle
- Debit card and backup debit card
- Emergency cash
- Other ....

Stuff to Wear

- Underwear
- Socks
- Bottoms
- Tops
- Sweaters
- Dresses and pants
- Waterproof jacket
- Swimsuit
- Jacket
- Watch
- Flip-flops
- Sneakers
- Hiking boots
- Casual shoes
- Hat
- Sunglasses
- Gloves
- Workout clothes
- Belt
- Other ....

Toiletries and Health-Related Items

- Medications
- Hand sanitizer
- First aid kit
- Toothbrush, toothpaste, dental floss
- Mouthwash
- Hairbrush/comb
- Insect repellant
- Period products
- Vitamins
- Cotton swabs
- Tissues
- Sunscreen and after-sun lotion
- Baby wipes
- Tweezers
- Body wash
- Contact lenses and saline solution
- Shampoo and conditioner
- Shaving stuff
- Other

Little Extras

- Mini lint roller
- Laundry pen/stain remover
- Portable battery pack
- Flashlight
- Umbrella
- Mini sewing kit
- Other

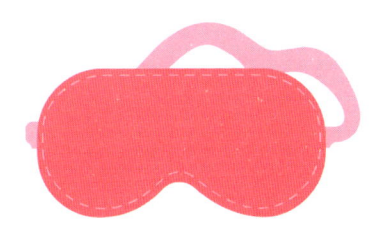

REFLECTIONS

Why I picked this trip:

When I set off on my trip I felt:

The places I went looked like:

The places I went smelled like:

The best thing(s) I ate:

The best thing(s) I saw:

The best thing(s) I did:

The best place(s) I went:

Things I experienced for the first time:

Things that surprised me:

Things that inspired me:

Things that challenged me:

Things that made me laugh:

The most exciting part of my trip:

I really appreciated it when:

I felt the happiest when:

One thing I did that I wasn't planning on doing:

One thing I did that was way better than I expected:

Some important things I learned:

Souvenirs I bought on my trip:

The most interesting people I met:

One thing that put me out of my comfort zone:

One thing that reminded me of home:

This trip made me grateful for:

How I felt about leaving:

What I discovered about myself:

What I'd do differently if I could take this trip again:

How this trip changed me for the better:

Other notes:

TRIP PLANNER

Trip Name:
Where:
When:
With Whom:
Weather:

My Itinerary:

PACKING LIST

The Basic Stuff

- [ ] Travel docs
- [ ] This journal
- [ ] Reading material
- [ ] Travel pillow
- [ ] Sleeping mask
- [ ] Headphones
- [ ] Earplugs
- [ ] Phone charger
- [ ] Pen
- [ ] Eyeglasses
- [ ] Travel lock
- [ ] Snacks
- [ ] Chewing gum
- [ ] Universal adaptor
- [ ] Reusable straw
- [ ] Reusable water bottle
- [ ] Debit card and backup debit card
- [ ] Emergency cash
- [ ] Other ....
- [ ] ....
- [ ] ....
- [ ] ....
- [ ] ....

Stuff to Wear

- [ ] Underwear
- [ ] Socks
- [ ] Bottoms
- [ ] Tops
- [ ] Sweaters
- [ ] Dresses and pants
- [ ] Waterproof jacket
- [ ] Swimsuit
- [ ] Jacket
- [ ] Watch
- [ ] Flip-flops
- [ ] Sneakers
- [ ] Hiking boots
- [ ] Casual shoes
- [ ] Hat
- [ ] Sunglasses
- [ ] Gloves
- [ ] Workout clothes
- [ ] Belt
- [ ] Other ....
- [ ] ....
- [ ] ....
- [ ] ....

Toiletries and Health-Related Items

- Medications
- Hand sanitizer
- First aid kit
- Toothbrush, toothpaste, dental floss
- Mouthwash
- Hairbrush/comb
- Insect repellant
- Period products
- Vitamins
- Cotton swabs
- Tissues
- Sunscreen and after-sun lotion
- Baby wipes
- Tweezers
- Body wash
- Contact lenses and saline solution
- Shampoo and conditioner
- Shaving stuff
- Other

Little Extras

- Mini lint roller
- Laundry pen/stain remover
- Portable battery pack
- Flashlight
- Umbrella
- Mini sewing kit
- Other

REFLECTIONS

Why I picked this trip:

When I set off on my trip I felt:

The places I went looked like:

The places I went smelled like:

The best thing(s) I ate:

The best thing(s) I saw:

The best thing(s) I did:

The best place(s) I went:

Things I experienced for the first time:

Things that surprised me:

Things that inspired me:

Things that challenged me:

Things that made me laugh:

The most exciting part of my trip:

I really appreciated it when:

I felt the happiest when:

One thing I did that I wasn't planning on doing:

One thing I did that was way better than I expected:

Some important things I learned:

Souvenirs I bought on my trip:

The most interesting people I met:

One thing that put me out of my comfort zone:

One thing that reminded me of home:

This trip made me grateful for:

How I felt about leaving:

What I discovered about myself:

What I'd do differently if I could take this trip again:

How this trip changed me for the better:

Other notes:

TRIP PLANNER

Trip Name: ....
Where: ....
When: ....
With Whom: ....
Weather: ....

My Itinerary: ....
....
....
....
....
....
....
....
....
....
....
....
....
....
....
....
....
....
....
....

PACKING LIST

The Basic Stuff

- Travel docs
- This journal
- Reading material
- Travel pillow
- Sleeping mask
- Headphones
- Earplugs
- Phone charger
- Pen
- Eyeglasses
- Travel lock
- Snacks
- Chewing gum
- Universal adaptor
- Reusable straw
- Reusable water bottle
- Debit card and backup debit card
- Emergency cash
- Other

Stuff to Wear

- Underwear
- Socks
- Bottoms
- Tops
- Sweaters
- Dresses and pants
- Waterproof jacket
- Swimsuit
- Jacket
- Watch
- Flip-flops
- Sneakers
- Hiking boots
- Casual shoes
- Hat
- Sunglasses
- Gloves
- Workout clothes
- Belt
- Other

Toiletries and Health-Related Items

- Medications
- Hand sanitizer
- First aid kit
- Toothbrush, toothpaste, dental floss
- Mouthwash
- Hairbrush/comb
- Insect repellant
- Period products
- Vitamins
- Cotton swabs
- Tissues
- Sunscreen and after-sun lotion
- Baby wipes
- Tweezers
- Body wash
- Contact lenses and saline solution
- Shampoo and conditioner
- Shaving stuff
- Other

Little Extras

- Mini lint roller
- Laundry pen/stain remover
- Portable battery pack
- Flashlight
- Umbrella
- Mini sewing kit
- Other

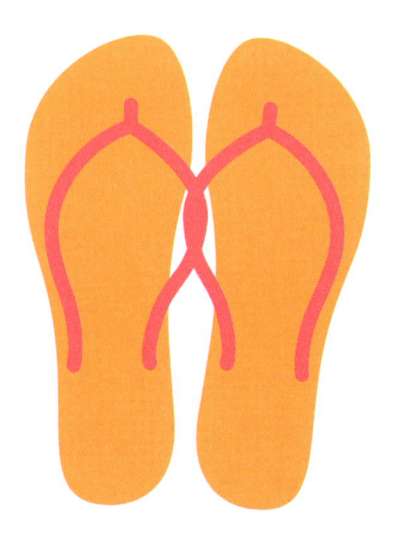

REFLECTIONS

Why I picked this trip:

When I set off on my trip I felt:

The places I went looked like:

The places I went smelled like:

The best thing(s) I ate:

The best thing(s) I saw:

The best thing(s) I did:

The best place(s) I went:

Things I experienced for the first time:

Things that surprised me:

Things that inspired me:

Things that challenged me:

Things that made me laugh:

The most exciting part of my trip:

I really appreciated it when:

I felt the happiest when:

One thing I did that I wasn't planning on doing:

One thing I did that was way better than I expected:

Some important things I learned:

Souvenirs I bought on my trip:

The most interesting people I met:

One thing that put me out of my comfort zone:

One thing that reminded me of home:

This trip made me grateful for:

How I felt about leaving:

What I discovered about myself:

What I'd do differently if I could take this trip again:

How this trip changed me for the better:

Other notes:

TRIP PLANNER

Trip Name: ....
Where: ....
When: ....
With Whom: ....
Weather: ....

My Itinerary: ....
....
....
....
....
....
....
....
....
....
....
....
....
....
....

PACKING LIST

The Basic Stuff

- Travel docs
- This journal
- Reading material
- Travel pillow
- Sleeping mask
- Headphones
- Earplugs
- Phone charger
- Pen
- Eyeglasses
- Travel lock
- Snacks
- Chewing gum
- Universal adaptor
- Reusable straw
- Reusable water bottle
- Debit card and backup debit card
- Emergency cash
- Other . . . .
- . . . .
- . . . .
- . . . .

Stuff to Wear

- Underwear
- Socks
- Bottoms
- Tops
- Sweaters
- Dresses and pants
- Waterproof jacket
- Swimsuit
- Jacket
- Watch
- Flip-flops
- Sneakers
- Hiking boots
- Casual shoes
- Hat
- Sunglasses
- Gloves
- Workout clothes
- Belt
- Other . . . .
- . . . .
- . . . .
- . . . .

Toiletries and Health-Related Items

Medications

Hand sanitizer

First aid kit

Toothbrush, toothpaste, dental floss

Mouthwash

Hairbrush/comb

Insect repellant

Period products

Vitamins

Cotton swabs

Tissues

Sunscreen and after-sun lotion

Baby wipes

Tweezers

Body wash

Contact lenses and saline solution

Shampoo and conditioner

Shaving stuff

Other

Little Extras

Mini lint roller

Laundry pen/stain remover

Portable battery pack

Flashlight

Umbrella

Mini sewing kit

Other

REFLECTIONS

Why I picked this trip:

When I set off on my trip I felt:

The places I went looked like:

The places I went smelled like:

The best thing(s) I ate:

The best thing(s) I saw:

The best thing(s) I did:

The best place(s) I went:

Things I experienced for the first time:

Things that surprised me:

Things that inspired me:

Things that challenged me:

Things that made me laugh:

The most exciting part of my trip:

I really appreciated it when:

I felt the happiest when:

One thing I did that I wasn't planning on doing:

One thing I did that was way better than I expected:

Some important things I learned:

Souvenirs I bought on my trip:

The most interesting people I met:

One thing that put me out of my comfort zone:

One thing that reminded me of home:

This trip made me grateful for:

How I felt about leaving:

What I discovered about myself:

What I'd do differently if I could take this trip again:

How this trip changed me for the better:

Other notes:

ADJECTIVE WHEELS

If you're feeling at a loss for words as you record, write, and reflect on your travels and trips, use the following adjective wheels to help describe what you're seeing, doing, or feeling.

"Traveling—it leaves you speechless, then turns you into a storyteller."

—Ibn Battuta, scholar and explorer

HAPPY

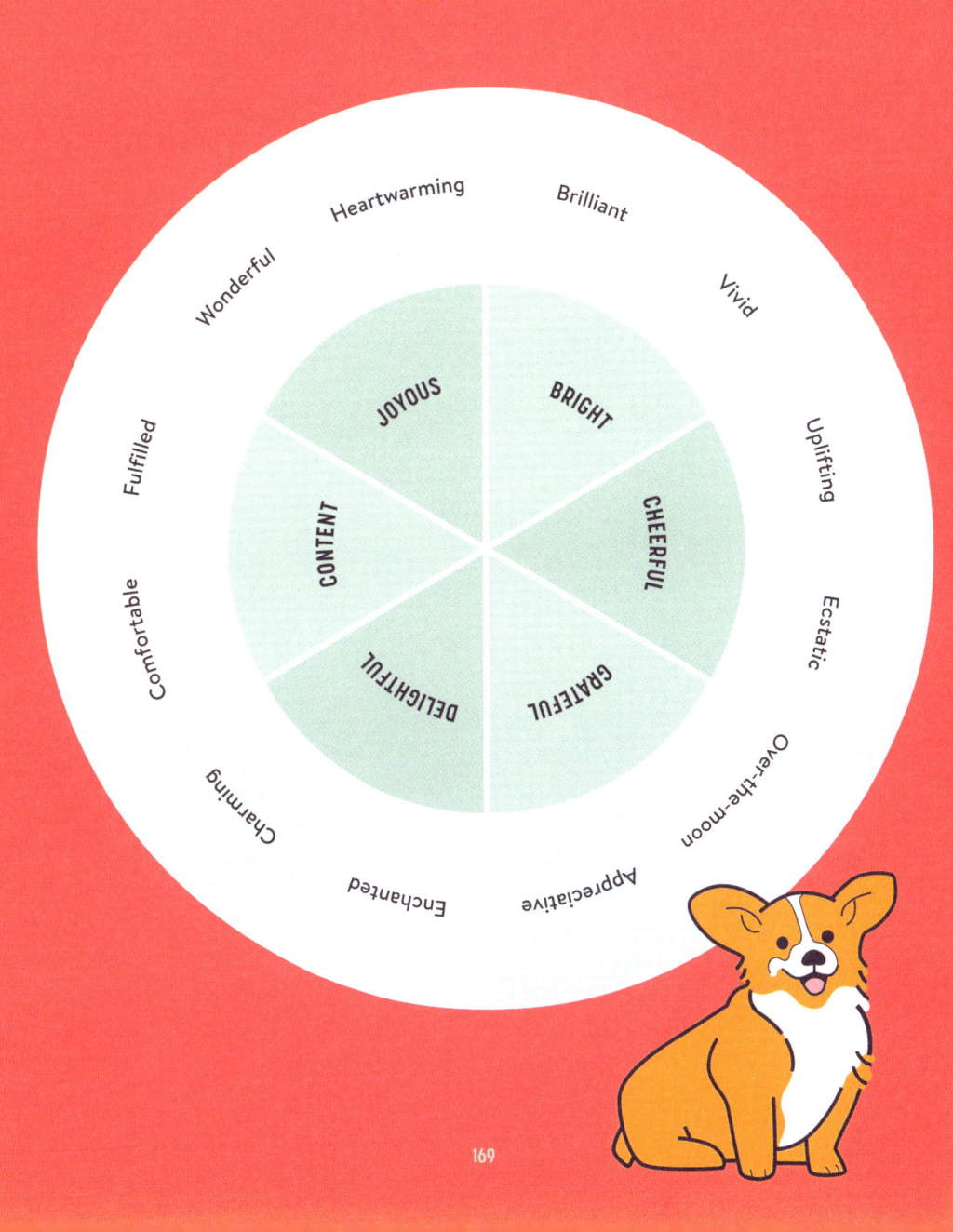

- Heartwarming
- Brilliant
- Wonderful
- Vivid
- Fulfilled
- Uplifting
- Comfortable
- Ecstatic
- Charming
- Over-the-moon
- Enchanted
- Appreciative

JOYOUS · **BRIGHT** · **CHEERFUL** · **GRATEFUL** · **DELIGHTFUL** · **CONTENT**

TASTY

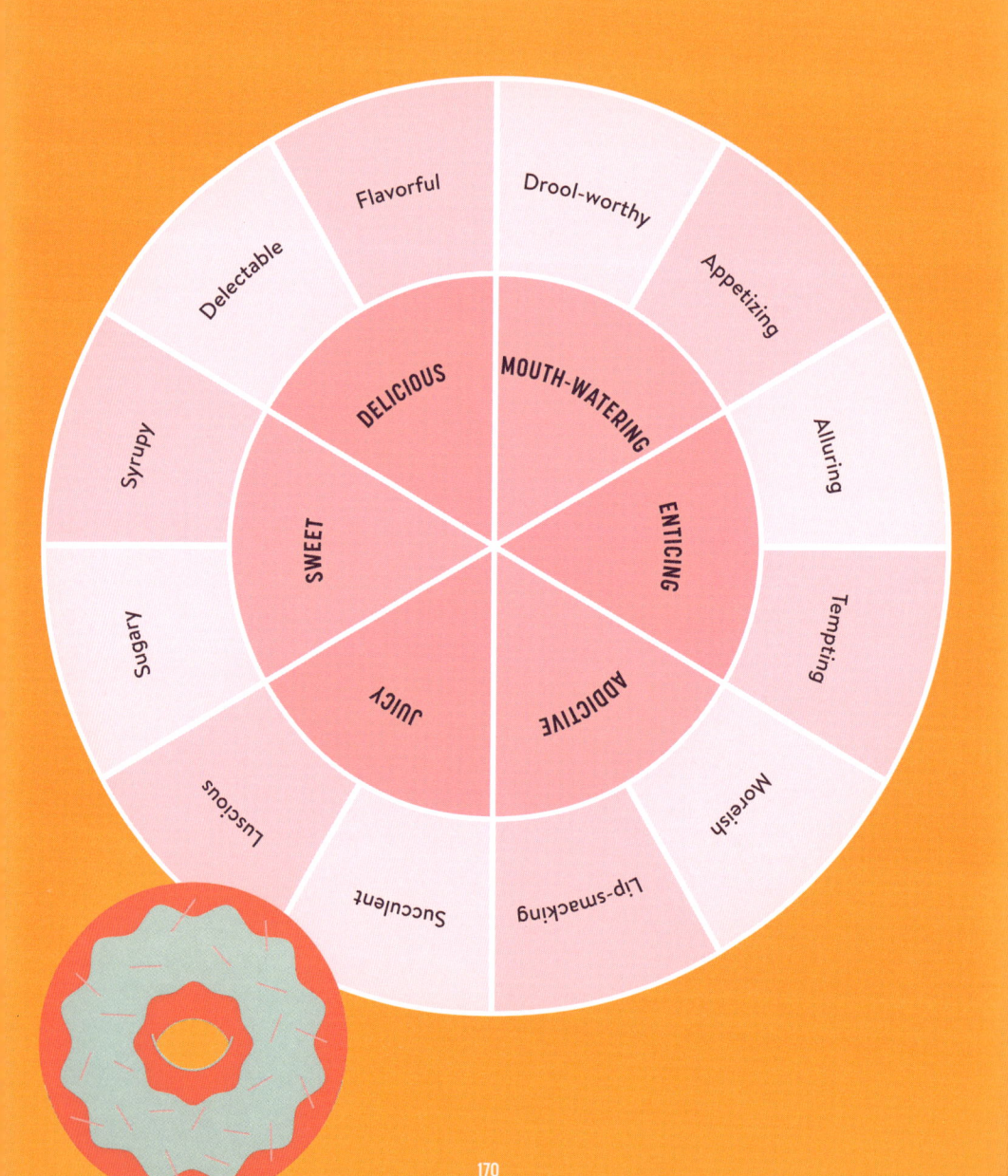

- **DELICIOUS**
  - Flavorful
  - Delectable
- **MOUTH-WATERING**
  - Drool-worthy
  - Appetizing
- **ENTICING**
  - Alluring
  - Tempting
- **ADDICTIVE**
  - Moreish
  - Lip-smacking
- **JUICY**
  - Succulent
  - Luscious
- **SWEET**
  - Sugary
  - Syrupy

SURPRISING

- **UNIQUE**
  - Bizarre
  - Unusual
- **ARRESTING**
  - Over-whelming
  - Staggering
- **INCREDIBLE**
  - Astonishing
  - Unbelievable
- **IMPRESSIVE**
  - Mind-blowing
  - Intense
- **INTERESTING**
  - Fascinating
  - Curious
- **SCARY**
  - Shocking
  - Thrilling

PRETTY

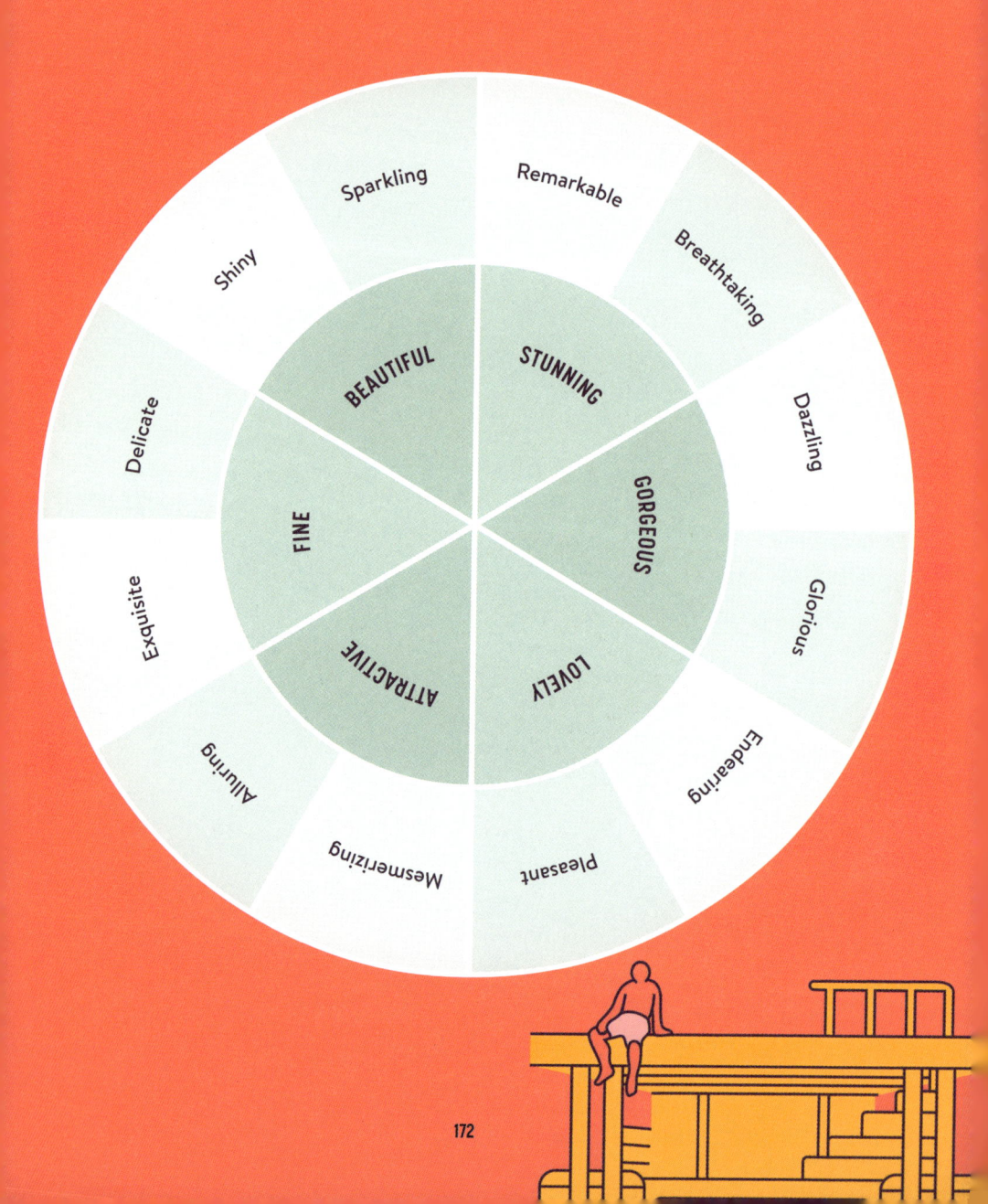

- Sparkling
- Remarkable
- Breathtaking
- Shiny
- Dazzling
- Delicate
- Glorious
- Exquisite
- Endearing
- Alluring
- Pleasant
- Mesmerizing

BEAUTIFUL · **STUNNING** · **GORGEOUS** · **LOVELY** · **ATTRACTIVE** · **FINE**

COOL

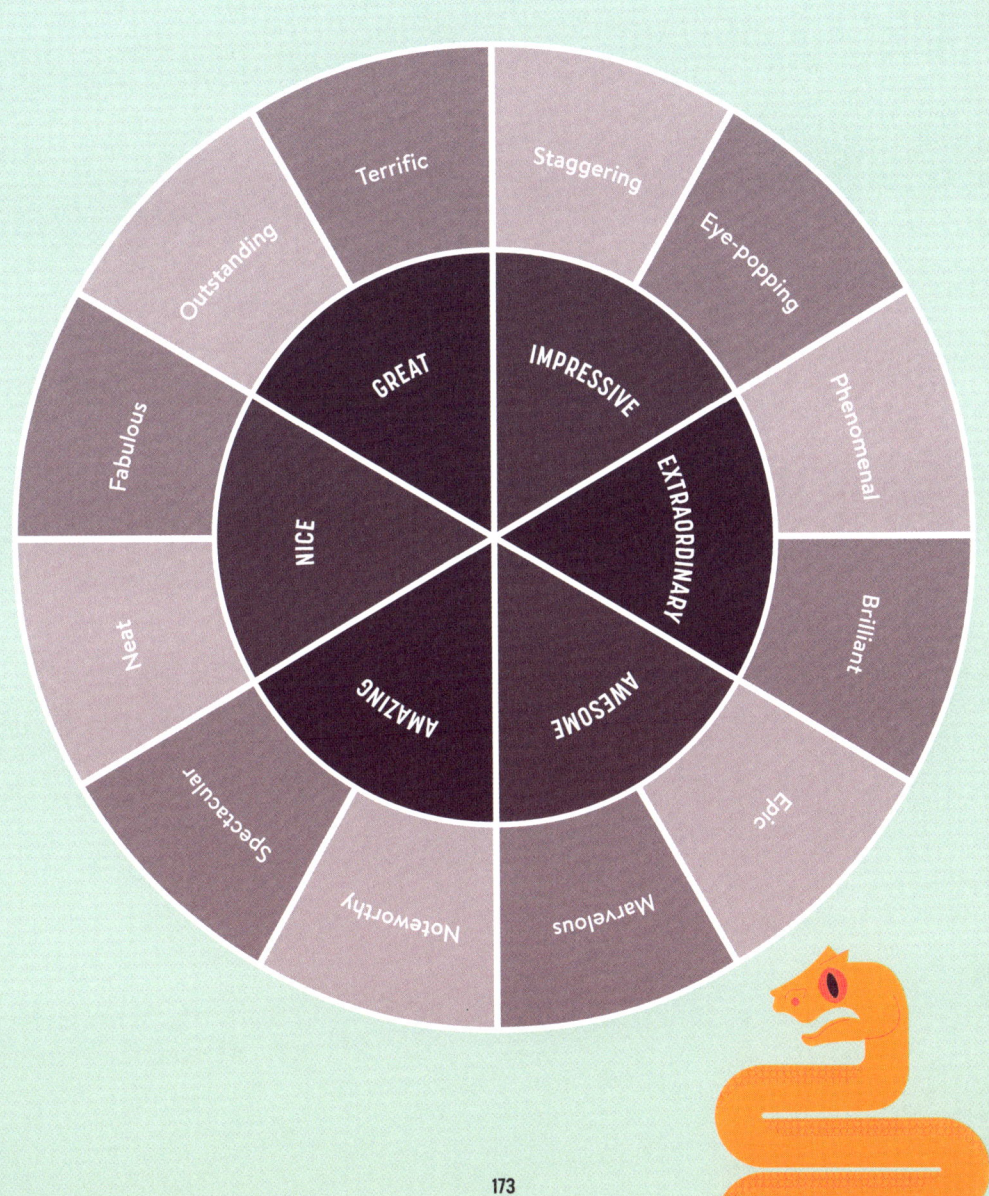

- NICE
  - Terrific
  - Outstanding
  - Fabulous
  - Neat
- GREAT
- IMPRESSIVE
  - Staggering
  - Eye-popping
- EXTRAORDINARY
  - Phenomenal
  - Brilliant
- AWESOME
  - Epic
  - Marvelous
- AMAZING
  - Noteworthy
  - Spectacular

FUN

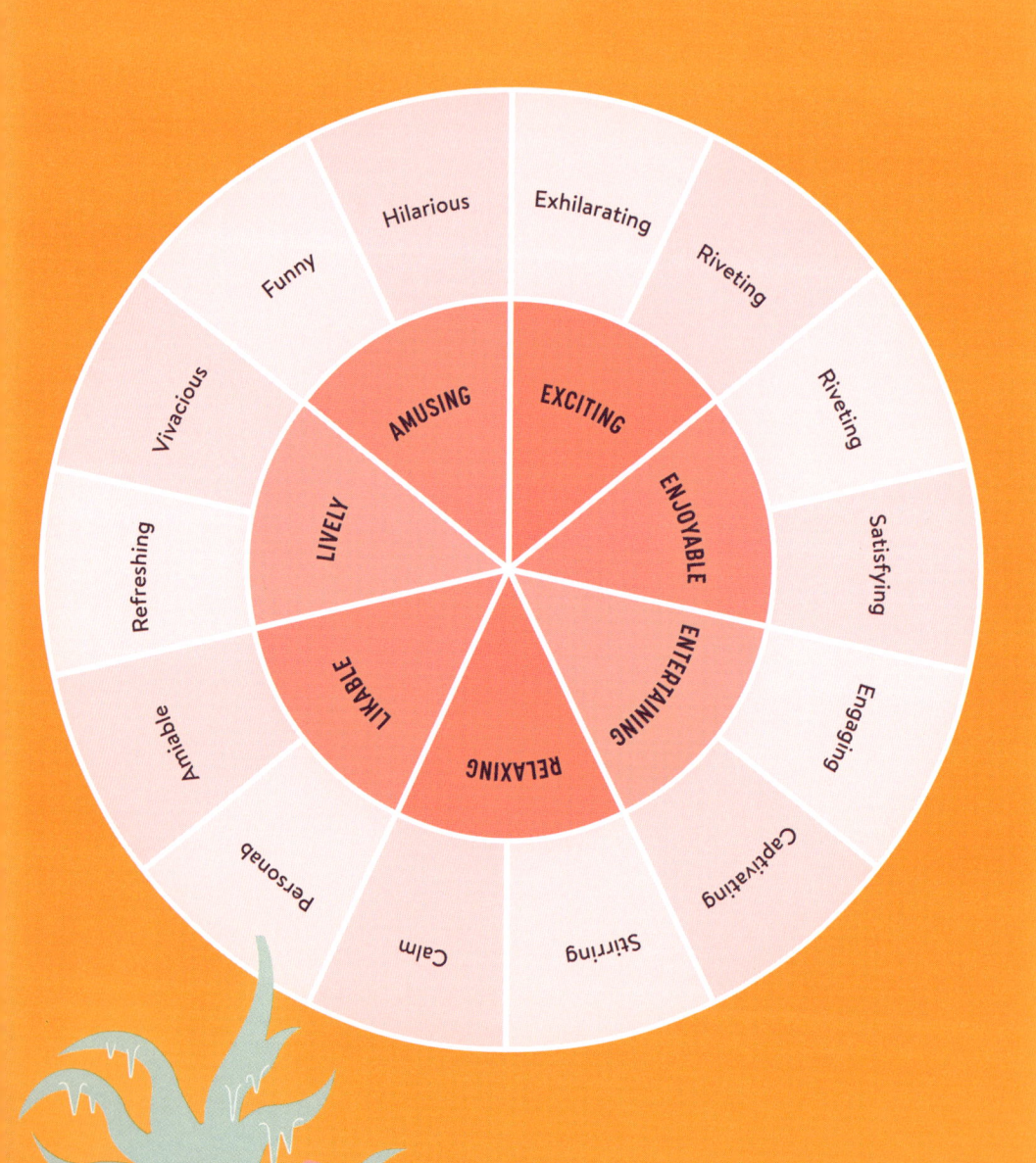

- AMUSING
  - Hilarious
  - Funny
- EXCITING
  - Exhilarating
  - Riveting
- ENJOYABLE
  - Riveting
  - Satisfying
- ENTERTAINING
  - Engaging
  - Captivating
- RELAXING
  - Stirring
  - Calm
- LIKABLE
  - Personab[le]
  - Amiable
- LIVELY
  - Refreshing
  - Vivacious

NOTES